Aspects of modern sociology

Social structure of modern Britain

GENERAL EDITORS

John Barron Mays
Eleanor Rathbone Professor of Sociology, University of Liverpool

Maurice Craft
Goldsmiths' Professor of Education, University of London

Education

Ronald King, M.Sc., Ph.D.

Reader in Education
University of Exeter

Second edition

Longman
London and New York

Longman Group Limited London

Associated companies, branches and representatives
throughout the world

First edition published in the United States of America
by Humanities Press
Second edition published in the United States of America
by Longman Inc., New York

© Longman Group Limited 1969, 1977

First published 1969
Second edition 1977

Library of Congress Cataloging in Publication Data

King, Ronald, 1934–
  Education

  (Aspects of modern sociology)
  Bibliography: p.
  Includes index.
  1. Education – Great Britain – 1965 –   I. Title.
LA632.K5 1977   370′.941   77-1388
ISBN 0–582–48550–9

Printed in Great Britain by
Lowe & Brydone Printers Limited, Thetford

Contents

Editors' preface

This series has been designed to meet the needs of students following a variety of academic and professional courses in universities, polytechnics, colleges of higher education, colleges of education, and colleges of further education. Although principally of interest to social scientists, the series does not attempt a comprehensive treatment of the whole field of sociology, but concentrates on the social structure of modern Britain which forms a central feature of most such tertiary level courses in this country. Its purpose is to offer an analysis of our contemporary society through the study of basic demographic, ideological and structural features, and the examination of such major social institutions as the family, education, the economic and political structure, and religion. The aim has been to produce a series of introductory texts which will in combination form the basis for a sustained course of study, but each volume has been designed as a single whole and can be read in its own right.

We hope that the topics covered in the series will prove attractive to a wide reading public and that, in addition to students, others who wish to know more than is readily available about the nature and structure of their own society will find them of interest.

JOHN BARRON MAYS
MAURICE CRAFT

Foreword to the second edition

It is nearly ten years since I started to write the first edition of this book. Since then three important sets of changes have occurred the extent of which required the virtual rewriting of this new edition. Firstly, the many changes in educational institutions, organisations, policies and practices. Secondly, there has been a great deal more research in education. Thirdly, changes have occurred among sociologists of education, who have become more concerned with sociological theory. I make few references to the ongoing debate about the nature of the sociology of education that this has engendered, not because it is unimportant, but because it is being dealt with extensively elsewhere. However, some of the awarenesses created by this debate are indicated in the discussion of some of the research studies referred to. Furthermore, no one can write about education without the use of some kind of theoretical stance, however implicit. The references to Weber indicate my disposition towards theories of action and conflict, and my recognition of the importance of ideas in social life.

As with the first edition I hope that this new edition conveys some of my own fascination in the study of British education, and the contribution that sociology has made to that study, although there is still much to be done.

Education and society 1

Education in modern Britain is a large-scale activity. Virtually all adult members of British society have experienced nine or more years of full-time education. About one-sixth of the total population are currently receiving full-time education. This includes nearly all the children between the ages of five and sixteen; altogether more than 9 million in England and Wales. In addition nearly 4 million young and mature adults are engaged in full or part-time education. The processes of education, including administration, teaching and the ancillary services, are staffed by nearly a million workers; more than the labour force of the iron and steel industry. Twelve per cent of public expenditure goes to the education service; more than the amount spent on either defence or the health and social services. This large-scale commitment of both money and manpower is an index of the importance placed on education in this country, and this importance is explained and justified in a number of different ways.

Education as cultural transmission

The term culture is not used evaluatively to refer to personal taste in music or the arts but in a technical sense. Culture is the totality of shared, learned behaviour, according to which members of society live. The culture of a society has qualities which make it recognisably different from that of other societies, and includes skills, knowledge and techniques, beliefs, ideas and values which guide the actions of everyday life.

Small and simple societies tend to have a traditional and largely unchanging culture which is transmitted through the family or tribal system. In larger and more complex societies such as modern Britain cultural change is a continuous process and the traditional agencies of cultural transmission, particularly the family, are supplemented by an established educational system, as well as by reading, the mass media, and voluntary associations such as youth clubs and the Boy Scout movement.

The culture that is transmitted by the educational system is related to that of the culture of the wider society, but it is not identical to it. This is partly because it is mainly transmitted to children, and it is considered that some aspects of adult culture may be harmful or distressing to them, or may be difficult for them to understand. The knowledge transmitted to children is therefore a modified, even idealised, selection of that available. Sex education has been generally neglected in Britain, partly because the sexual aspects of adult behaviour are not considered suitable knowledge for young children. Other aspects of adult life about which there is little general consensus, for example, politics, may also be selected out. Others may be presented only obliquely. For example, the study of Henry VIII may be the only time that either divorce or the Catholic/Protestant distinction are discussed in school. In addition, the total knowledge content in a large complex society is enormous. No one person could know it all. The knowledge transmitted through education is therefore a selection of that available (Lawton, 1975, ch. 4).*

The idea of education as cultural transmission applies particularly to the education that most children receive in their primary schools. This includes the acquisition of the basic skills of number and literacy, which, despite the existence of some illiterate millionaires, can be considered to be prerequisites for competence in adult life. It also includes the transmission of ideas about the nature of being British and the place of Britain in

---

* Details of references are supplied in the annotated list at the end of this book, p. 146.

the world and in history. The partial nature of elementary geography is shown in the central position of this country in maps of the world. In French history books they won the battle of Waterloo.

Bernstein has made a useful distinction between the *instrumental* and *expressive* cultural components of the educational process; the former refers to 'the acquisition of specific skills', the latter to the transmission of models of, 'conduct, character and manner' (Bernstein *et al.*, 1971). This analysis of the duality of the educational process has many parallels. In common speech we make a distinction between two meanings of the word 'good', either in the sense of being skilful and accomplished, or in being morally and socially amenable. Lacey (1970) has shown how teachers used 'good' in connection with both a pupil's work and behaviour. A similar distinction is made by headteachers when they refer to 'academic' and 'social' education (King, 1973).

Two further aspects of education as cultural transmission should be pointed out. Firstly, the idea implies the notion of cultural consensus, that there is general agreement about appropriate ways of thinking and behaving, and about beliefs and values. Although it may be argued that there does exist such a 'mainstream' culture, there is the view that modern Britain also contains social groups with many different styles of life which constitute fairly distinct subcultures. These subcultural groups include those based on social class, region, religion and ethnic character. There are many different ways of being British.

Secondly, the process of cultural transmission in the here and now is concerned with the competence of children to cope with tasks and expectations set by their teachers. Competence in school is assumed to lead to competence in adult life. This is expressed in the phrase 'the school as a society'.

Education and occupation

All children eventually leave the educational system to enter occupations. The link between education and occupation is based on a closely related set of ideas. Firstly, that children vary in their ability to do school work. The use of intelligence and other tests by educational psychologists are attempts to put precision to this idea, as are school and public examinations. Tests are constructed in such a way as to make the assumption of a normal distribution of ability – that there are a few bright children, most are average, and a few are dull – actually come true. Similarly, examinations are marked in such a way that a fairly fixed quota of candidates pass, fail, get good or poor grades (Esland, 1971). Tests and examinations are part of what has been called the selection function of education, or more romantically, the creation of talent.

There are more than 50,000 different occupations in modern Britain, and the number is increasing. The assumption is made that certain levels and types of abilities are essential prerequisites for adequate performance in particular jobs. In general those with the higher social honour and higher wages are considered to require higher levels of ability expressed in higher levels of examination success (Collins, 1972). This has been called the allocation function of education, although it should be noted that a particular level of qualification does not lead to occupational placement but creates eligibility for certain occupations. The idea that the 'cleverest' should have the most desirable jobs is part of the idea of a meritocracy (Young, 1961).

When employers and different occupational groups select new members on the basis of their educational qualifications they effectively prevent the possibility of a person without such qualifications showing that he or she could do the job adequately. Bogus doctors are revealed from time to time, usually because their paper credentials are suspected rather than through incompetence. Until recently there existed a large number of adequate teachers with no teaching qualifications at all. Occupational groups may be seen as being in competition for the scarce resources of power, social honour and wages. There are more than 200 occupational qualifying associations active in this way. The linking of occupational status to the educational status of its members means that education is also a scarce resource for which individuals and occupational groups compete.

This calculative importance of education is shown in the results of a number of surveys of older pupils and their parents who see the school as an avenue to the occupational structure. In a survey by King (1973) of over 7,000 secondary schools pupils 94 per cent agreed that 'the main reason for working hard is to get a good job', and 88 per cent agreed that, 'passing exams is the way to get on'.

Such sentiments are sometimes deplored by teachers who feel that they devalue education, but it should be pointed out that the occupational rewards of exam success are commonly used by teachers to motivate their older pupils. It is clear that much of what is learnt in school has little direct relevance to many occupations; a bank clerk may have obtained the job on the basis of O levels in chemistry, English literature and religious knowledge. Most skills are learnt on the job. It could be argued that the existence of many non-vocational studies depends on such illogicalities. Perhaps teachers of English literature should be content to have the opportunity to present their pupils with the experience of poetry even if their main motivation is to get another O level leading to a job where they will not need to know an allegory from an apostrophe.

Despite the dubious aspects of this link between education and occupation the alternative methods of job placement might be considered to be less desirable. Leaving aside Marx's dream of men doing whatever work they choose, these include the use of patronage, the purchase and inheritance of positions, nepotism and direction by the state. These were common in the past and are still in use. It would be wrong to overstate the importance of qualifications in job placement. Many positions are filled on the basis of family connections; in many situations there are advantages in being the boss's son, or son-in-law. T. H. Marshall (1963) wrote: 'The ticket obtained on leaving school or college is a ticket for a life journey'. Some do not need tickets to travel far: they travel free.

Related to the linking of education and occupation is the specialisation of the education of older children and students. This is evident in the vocational courses in secondary schools and technical colleges, and in the training of doctors and engineers, where specialised knowledge fairly clearly related to the particular job is transmitted, together with models of appropriate behaviour, for example, the doctor's demeanour with patients. In addition, certain forms of learning and kinds of knowledge are assumed to be suitable for children of different abilities and therefore different occupational destinies. High status knowledge is found in books and is assessed by written exams, and includes subjects without obvious direct practical application, such as English literature, Latin and history. Low status knowledge is hand work involving materials and a stress on non-verbal skills, and includes the craft subjects (Young, 1971).

Two other aspects of the relationship between education and occupation should be briefly mentioned. Children kept in school until at least sixteen cannot go to work; the number of low skill jobs traditionally followed by young unqualified people has fallen. When their children are at school mothers find it easier to go out to work; about 40 per cent with children of school age do so.

Education and the economy

Ideas about the relationship between education and the economy have changed radically over a short period of time. The Crowther Committee (1959) saw a fairly simple functional relationship, referring to the need 'to provide an adequate supply of brains and skill to sustain economic productivity'. This view of education as an investment industry was used to justify educational expansion which would therefore benefit both the individual and society. It is more difficult to sustain in a situation where money is less plentiful and where the graduate scientists industry was supposed to be seeking are sometimes unemployed. Woodhall and Blaug (1968) made an input–output analysis of secondary education for 1950–63 and concluded its productivity had declined during this period of expansion. Education was judged to have taken more out of the economy than it put back.

The relationship between education and the economy is a complex one. Collins (1972) has concluded that the only reasonably certain connection between the level of education and economic growth is in the operation of a threshold level in terms of universal basic literacy and numeracy. What is clear is that education is being judged more and more on the basis of the expenditure it involves, rather than any national profit it may make.

Education and social class

Modern Britain is a highly industrialised, complex society. In modern industrialised societies occupational positions tend to assume a greater importance than family ones. The tendency when meeting someone new is to find out what his job is, not his family connections. This is because occupation provides the most useful single indication of the kind of life a person leads, his *life-style*.

The social structure of modern Britain is described as stratified because groups of similar occupations in terms of training, entrance qualifications, conditions of work and wages, are given a fairly distinct social position or status. This stratified structure is not regulated by laws, as were the estates of medieval times, or by ritual, as are the castes of India, but is based on the way that the different members of society regard their own social position and that of others. This is a *social class* structure. By its very nature such a structure is difficult to define and describe because one of its essential features is that there are no sharp divisions between the social classes. Furthermore, the class structure is a dynamic one in that a man may change his occupation, or an occupation may change its characteristics, and therefore there is a movement between the classes, called *social mobility*.

Phrases like 'the social class system is dead', or 'we are all middle class now', have political usage in Britain but are non-sense when the term class is used in the technical sense. To some degree all typologies of class are arbitrary. In this book the terms 'middle classes' and 'working classes' will be frequently used. The middle classes are those occupations which are essentially non-manual in character: the professional, managerial, clerical and other white collar workers. They work with their heads, in 'clean' jobs, possibly gained through educational qualifications, and receive a monthly salary. 'Working classes' are the skilled, semiskilled and unskilled manual workers. They work with their hands in 'dirty' jobs, sometimes gained through specialist training, and receive a weekly wage, on average less money than non-manual workers.

These terms are used as *ideal types*, that is, they describe collections of consistent social characteristics. (The treatment of class and ideal type in this section follows that of Weber more than any other theorist: see e.g. Worsley, 1970, and Thompson and Tunstall, 1971.) There is, however, considerable variation in characteristics not only between the classes but also within them. It is therefore important to realise the limitations of generalisations about the middle and working classes. It is also important to remember that particular individuals may not completely fit any general description. Indeed, there will be a few who do not fit at all. Moreover many individuals dissent from the way they are classified by occupation, although most people in this country agree there are social classes and classify occupations in much the same way (Martin, 1954).

How do children, who are not part of the occupational structure, fit into this discussion? References to working-class or middle-class children use the fathers' occupation as the basis for the classification (wives are usually given their husbands' status for analytical purposes). The justification for this is largely empirical in that a great deal of research, some to be quoted in later chapters, has shown many variations in the social characteristics of groups of children classified by their fathers' occupation. The work of the Newsons (1965, 1968, 1976) in Nottingham documents hundreds of these differences ranging from when they are put to bed to how much pocket money they get. (On average the middle-class children are put to bed earlier and get less pocket money.) The implication of this kind of study is that the nature of a man's occupation is closely related not only to the housing conditions of his family and the way the household budget is managed, but also to his relations with his wife and children.

For the Victorians the link between education and social class was quite explicit. Different kinds of school providing different kinds of education for different lengths of time were available to children of different social classes. At the extremes of the social order, the sons of the upper classes and the newly emergent prosperous middle class received a classical education at public schools lasting until they were in their teens (Mitchell, 1964). After the 1870 Education Act most of the children of the 'labouring classes' received instruction in the three Rs in elementary schools until they were twelve. The class connection was sometimes part of the name of the school, as in the Mayo Middle Class School for Girls in London (Campbell, 1956). The public schools still exist and continue to illustrate one purpose of education in confirming social status, in that their pupils are predominantly of the moneyed professional and managerial classes, both in terms of families of origin and occupational destinies (Kalton, 1966). For many their education is a symbol of their social status: being 'educated' is part of their way of life. The schools of the maintained sector of education receive children from all social backgrounds, although as later chapters will show they may vary a great deal in their social composition. As the next section shows, the outcome of maintained education may now be both *status conferring* and *status confirming*.

A certain amount of social mobility is inherent in a social class structure. Movement between the social classes may be accomplished in different ways. As a wife takes her husband's social status, a girl may change her status by marriage. This is *marriage mobility*: 'marrying up' or 'marrying down'. A man may change his job during the course of his working life; this is *career mobility*. In recent times the extent of career mobility seems to have declined and more *intergenerational mobility* is evident. This refers to a son taking a job of different status to that of his father. Upward intergeneration mobility in Britain is sometimes accomplished by the son receiving an extended education and acquiring qualifications leading to a higher status occupation. Many teachers are working-class in origin and are therefore examples of this kind of mobility (Floud and Scott, 1961). Education is often valued as a way of 'getting on', and this is based on its link with occupation in the way already discussed.

The rate of social mobility appears to be largely independent of the educational system; it is related to the nature of the occupational structure, where there has been an expansion of professional occupations and a reduction of unskilled ones. However, the method of selecting who should be upwardly mobile does appear to depend on the operation of the educational system. In the studies made by Glass (1954) and his associates in the postwar period, upward intergenerational mobility was often, but not always, associated with having been to grammar school. Successful working-class grammar school boys appear in many studies and are examples of education indirectly conferring new status (Jackson and Marsden, 1962). But educational failure may be associated with a middle-class experience of downward social mobility, another kind of conferred status, seldom written about. It should be stressed that for the majority of children education confirms their status, be they middle or working class.

Ralph Turner constructed two models representing different modes of upward social mobility through education. In *contest mobility*, high or elite status is *acquired* by contestants using a wide range of strategies over a long period of time. In *sponsored mobility*, recruits are selected for *ascribed* elite status by the members of the elite or their agents (Turner, 1961). The supposed criteria of merit for entry into the elite cannot be achieved by effort or strategy. Turner proposed that the American educational system approximated to the contest model, whilst that of Britain at the time of the Glass study approximated to the sponsored model. In America the comprehensive high school system and the ease of access into higher education, permit pupils and students to decide when they want their education to end, and they can if they wish resume their efforts to gain high status occupations. Until recently the only route to high status occupations provided by the maintained system of education in Britain was through the grammar school and then the higher education system. Access to this route was confined to a carefully selected minority. There were few second chances for those not selected (see chapter 6). Many of the recent changes in education, including the introduction of comprehensive schools, have been justified in terms of moves towards what is hoped to be a fairer contest system.

T. H. Marshall (1963), perhaps a little over-optimistically, neatly summarised the longer term changes in the idea, if not the practice, of the nature of education. In the nineteenth century it was, 'the education your status entitled you to', in the twentieth century, 'the status your education entitles you to'.

The control of education

The educational process is large-scale, expensive and regarded as important; not surprisingly it is subject to a wide range of controls. This exercise can be described in formal terms – who has the power to decide what; it is much more difficult to do it in functional terms – who actually decides and controls what. Educational power is not as strongly centralised at a governmental level as in France, and is less decentralised at the local level than the school boards of the USA. There are several loci of power.

At the national level, laws and statutory instruments are enacted by parliament on the initiative of the government. The Secretary of State for Education and Science is a member of the government, he or she decides policy and action in relation to education, and competes for the resources of money and parliamentary time among cabinet colleagues. The Secretary is the political head of the Department of Education and Science which is staffed by less powerful under secretaries of state and civil servants, the most important being the Permanent Under-Secretary of State. The DES sets minimum standards for education, controls the rate, cost and nature of educational building, and controls teacher supply and administers their salary scales. The DES is also concerned with rate support for the local education authorities, and may settle disputes in other sectors for example, between parents and LEAs. About 500 of Her Majesty's Inspectors report to the DES on their activities throughout the country (Burgess, 1972).

Only intimations of the actual working of the DES are available (Crosland and Boyle, 1971). The powerful resist research. As may be expected the party in power is an important element in policy at this level. Broadly speaking, Labour administrations compared with Conservative have been more favourable towards educational changes of an egalitarian kind, intended to distribute educational opportunities more equally, for example, in creating comprehensive schools, and more favourable towards educational expansion when economic conditions are judged to permit this. Secretaries of State come and go but the civil servants (metaphorically) go on for ever, and may act as powerful moderators of policy intentions, and decisive mediators of that policy (Kogan, 1975).

The 105 local education authorities have the duty to provide schools to DES standards, and ensure that parents send their children to school. They have the power to maintain or cease to maintain schools, and control the appointment of teachers. The political body of the LEA is the education committee, which like the DES at the national level, competes with other county committees for resources, especially money. Generally speaking Labour-controlled LEAs are more generous than Conservative ones (Boaden, 1973).

The Chief Education Officer is the permanent official of the

Committee. Miriam David (1973) in a study of LEAs identified two types of chief education officer. The conciliator types felt themselves to be primarily administrators and servants of the education committee in implementing its policy; the educator types are 'very evangelical and have a strong desire to develop and disseminate new ideas, methods and techniques in education'. The CEO is the head of the local education department which has its own permanent officers and local inspectors or advisers.

At the school level the most important position is that of the head-teacher, who in maintained (LEA) schools has legal responsibility for curriculum and discipline (King, 1968). These powerful persons are discussed in more detail later (chapters 5 and 9).

Most of the power exercised at the national, local and head-teacher level is based on the authority of law. Weber suggested that authority based on legal-rational legitimacy is expressed in the form of *bureaucratic control* (Weber, 1970). Bureaucracy is not used in a pejorative sense but refers to a number of related characteristics, including hierarchical control, clearly seen in the structure of the DES, local education departments and schools with the head-teacher at the top of the pyramid. Bureaucrats generate standardised procedures and rules. Apart from the law of education itself there are DES circulars and memoranda and LEA handbooks (Taylor and Saunders, 1971).

In schools bureaucratic control by the use of paper may be used by the head and the teachers, including rules, reports and syllabuses (see chapters 5 and 6). However, in many schools some of these have external origins – these are the public examinations. The high status O and A level General Certificate of Education (GCE) exams are under the main control of the university examining boards. The lower status Certificate of Secondary Education (CSE) is controlled by local boards with strong teacher representation. All public exams are also dealt with by the central Schools Council which has representatives from

LEAs, universities and teachers' unions, and like other powerful educational bodies has only been researched from the outside (Manzer, 1975; Young, 1975).

The form of education and what counts as *educational knowledge* are partly decided by those who have the legal authority to do so and the bureaucracy to implement their decisions. But the exercise of power in education also depends on the receipt of the legitimacy from at least two other sources. The importance of parents' legitimacy is usually shown when they do not approve, as in the case of the William Tyndale School where some parents withdrew their children because they were dissatisfied with the way they were being taught (Auld, 1976). The essential educational process takes place in classrooms. Despite the superstructure of laws, syllabuses, rules and contracts, the teacher's authority over her pupils rests on the receipt of their legitimation of her power over them. Research by King (1973) showed that the majority of pupils in most secondary schools approved of most of the things they were expected to do. This does not mean that conflict is not found in the classrooms in this country. A certain level occurs in most educational processes, but seldom leads to its breakdown, as in the pupil strikes of 1911 (Marson, 1973). The mysteries of social control in the classroom will be discussed later (chapters 5, 6 and 9).

In addition to those groups which have legal authority within education, other groups exist with particular interests in education; they seek acceptance of their ideas through membership of local and national committees, pamphlets, conferences, lobbying and petitions, with a view to their being implemented by those with the power to do so. These include more than twenty teachers' unions and associations, the largest being the National Union of Teachers, the parents' organisations including the Confederation for the Advancement of State Education, the denominational organisations such as the Church of England Board of Education, and about 700 others ranging from Advisory Centre for Education to the Zoological Society of London (*Education Committees Yearbook*). To these may be added individual ideologues, such as the contributors to the Black, White and Red Papers by Cox and Dyson (1969) ACE (1969) and Cuddity *et al,* (1970), in which debate sometimes becomes diatribe.

Two important observations emerge from this brief survey of the control of education. Firstly, that conflict and the competition for resources are endemic in education. Secondly, that there is no general consensus about the form, nature and purpose of education in this country. It is a common regret that education has anything to do with politics. Education is too important not to be a part of politics.

Education and social change

The consequences of education are sometimes obvious. That most people can read, write and do simple sums, that anyone knows any physics or French literature, is certainly mainly due to their having been to school or college. However if it were thought that the British had become more or less tolerant, more or less hard-working, it would be difficult to show these tendencies as outcomes of their education. Apart from their being difficult to define and measure, such things are also influenced by family, friends, reading and the mass media. Thus any discussion about the way education may change society tends to be highly general and rather vague.

However, it is clear that the official view of education in Victorian times was that it was to preserve the *status quo*. The opposite opinion, that education should be used to change society, is often denounced as *social engineering*, but using education to keep things as they are is also social engineering: maintenance rather than construction engineering.

To some extent this kind of discussion is based on a dubious distinction between education and society. This implies that children in school are not a part of society. But school is effectively the society of children. They spend at least eleven years

15

there, and they represent at least a tenth of the total population. Changes in education are changes in society. This point is returned to in the last chapter.

The different social classes in modern Britain are characterised by different life-styles, that is, patterns of expenditure and consumption, choice of amusements and pastimes and kinds of social relationships. These life-styles are indicated in the different *class chances* revealed by social surveys relating to all aspects of social life from birth to death. For example, the infant mortality rate among the children of unskilled manual workers is double that of those of professional workers (Nissel). Life-styles and class chances seem to be related, directly or indirectly, to occupation. The emphasis of studies in the sociology of education in Britain has been the investigation of the relationship between a child's education and his or her father's occupation, that is, class chances in education. The results of every survey show a consistent pattern, that of middle-class children on average having a longer educational life than working-class children. For example, the Douglas (1964) survey showed that a child of a professional or managerial father had about nine times more chance of getting a grammar school place than the child of a semiskilled or unskilled manual worker. Table 2.1 indicates the way these social class differentials continue in the careers of those pupils who did gain grammar school places.

Three important points should be made clear. Firstly, social class differences in educational attainment are not a uniquely British phenomenon. In every modern industrialised society that has been investigated a similar pattern has been found, not only in those with capitalist or mixed economies, but also, as far as the information allows, in communist Russia and China. Secondly, although the *proportion* of 'successful' working-class

Education

Table 2.1 *Achievement of grammar school pupils 1: (by percentage)*

Father's occupation	5 or more 'O' levels	2 or more 'A' levels	Degree level course
Non-manual	50	21	17
Manual	40	13	7

Source. Adapted from the Robbins Report (1963), App. One, Part 2, Table 5, p. 43.

children is lower, large *numbers* often are successful. About a third of all teachers, perhaps a fifth of a million, could be put into this category (see chapter 9). Thirdly, educational success is here being defined in instrumental terms, exam results and getting degrees, which ignores the other less easily defined and measurable expected outcomes of education, for example, tolerance.

A number of explanations or theories have been suggested to account for class differences in education.

Differential income theory

Although income is less tightly tied to social class than in the past, on average non-manual occupations still receive higher wages than manual, and the gap between the highest paid managers and the lowest paid unskilled workers is considerable (Nissel). (This ignores the social class distribution of capital.) The differential income theory poses that working-class children do less well at school because of their lower family income.

There is some evidence to support this theory. The children of the poor, mainly those from large families with unskilled manual worker fathers, sometimes have dietary and other deficiencies which may impair their learning abilities (Abel-Smith and Townsend 1965). The *Early Leaving* report (CAC, 1954) found that the predominantly working-class fifteen- and sixteen-year-old early leavers from grammar schools tended to come from overcrowded homes with what was judged to be inadequate provision for doing homework. Many left when a job was made available to them. The Social Survey of the Crowther Report (1960) showed that such job opportunities were commonly taken when the family income was low.

It was widely believed that the abolition of fees in maintained grammar schools after the 1944 Education Act would lead to an increased proportion of working-class pupils, but this did not happen. There is no denying the class differential in access to fee-paying private schools, but it has not been established that such schools confer advantages in terms of exam success. Douglas *et al* (1968) found that boys of the same social origins and measured intelligence did equally well in maintained grammar schools and independent schools.

This theory therefore probably has some validity in explaining the educational experience of children from the poorest homes, mainly 'lower' working class.

Differential provision theory

This can be summarised in the following three propositions: (*a*) working-class children have a poorer educational provision, (*b*) educational attainment is positively related to educational provision, and (*c*) the social class differences in educational attainment are (partly) explained by the differences in provision. Much evidence exists to support the first part of the theory. The report of the Public Schools Commission (1968) and the survey by Kalton (1966) both showed that the predominately middle-class pupils in the high status section of private education do have more money spent on them than pupils in maintained schools, as shown in smaller pupil/teacher ratios and better material facilities. Floud, Halsey and Martin (1957) found poorer material provision in the primary schools serving working class areas, and similar results were obtained for secondary modern schools in the surveys carried out for the Newsom Committee (CAC 1963) and by the National Union of Teachers.

However, the evidence to suggest a connection between

educational provision and attainment is not conclusive. Davies (1968), in an analysis of local education authorities, found that variations in expenditure per pupil, both in secondary and in primary schools, were small in relation to variations in attainment. More specifically, expenditures per secondary pupil were hardly correlated with the rate of staying on in school until the age of seventeen. The variations in the rates of staying on and of going on to higher education were, however, strongly related to high social class and the proportions of pupils in selective schools. Several studies have contradicted teachers' conventional wisdom in demonstrating higher attainment in larger size school classes (Little *et al*, 1971).

Byrne and Williamson (1975) made statistical explorations of the relationships between the educational expenditure, the rate of staying on at school, and the social composition of selected local authority areas. In line with expectation they found that middle-class areas are characterised by higher levels of educational expenditure and higher levels of staying on than working-class areas, and they claim that part of the variation in rates of staying on may be explained by the differences in educational expenditure. However, King (1974), in a study of a single LEA with high levels of expenditure, found that the neighbourhood comprehensive schools in working-class areas were the better provided for, as part of a policy of positive discrimination, but the average levels of attainment in these schools were still lower than those in middle-class areas. In the study of a single grammar school middle-class boys stayed on more frequently than working-class, having received the same overall provision (King, 1969).

It seems likely that the existing differences in educational provision make only a small contribution to class differences in attainment. (This is further discussed in the last chapter.)

Differential ability theory

This proposes that class differences in education and attainment are explained by differences in academic ability. Intelligence tests purport to measure such abilities, and the mean scores on such tests are higher for middle-class children than for working-class. Douglas (1964), using four tests, obtained a mean score of 110 for his upper middle-class group, 106 for the lower middle-class, 100 for the upper manual working-class, and 96 for lower manual working-class. It should be stressed that the variation in measured intelligence is greater within social classes than between them, and that using any reasonable definition of 'bright' and 'working' there are more bright working-class children than bright middle-class ones.

These class variations in measured intelligence do not however completely account for the variations in achievement between children of different social origins. Table 2.2 shows the rates of educational attainment for pupils from different backgrounds with the same measured intelligence.

Table 2.2 *Achievement of grammar school pupils: 2 (by percentage)*

I.Q. at 11+	Father's occupation	5 or more 'O' levels	2 or more 'A' levels	Degree level course
130 or more	Non-manual	73	43	37
	Manual	75	30	18
115–129	Non-manual	56	23	17
	Manual	45	14	8
100–114	Non-manual	37	9	6
	Manual	22	6	2

Source. As Table 2.1.

It is clear that educational achievement is associated with both higher measured intelligence and middle-class backgrounds. The middle-class background seems to be least advantageous to the most intelligent, and most advantageous to those with more modest measured intelligence. It can be seen that at all levels of measured intelligence middle-class pupils tend to 'overachieve' relative to working-class pupils. Furthermore the gap between the classes, in terms of achievement, tends to widen during the educational career. This *class gap* is widest among the 'less able' pupils.

The Hebb-Vernon model of intelligence breaks down the overall concept into three related parts (Vernon, 1960).

Intelligence A is the hypothesised, genetically determined, innate intelligence which is not (yet) measurable.

Intelligence B is that which develops as a result of the interaction of Intelligence A with the environment, that is, the socialisation process. The size and nature of Intelligence B will depend on Intelligence A and the nature of the socialisation process.

Intelligence C is a measure of Intelligence B. If the test is completely valid and reliable (which none are) then Intelligence C will equal Intelligence B.

There is no evidence to suggest that the hypothesised innate Intelligence A is distributed in any way but randomly across the population. The belief that members of the working class are genetically inferior with respect to intelligence has not been proved to be true; neither has it been proved to be false. If it is assumed that Intelligence C is approximately equal to Intelligence B, then measured intelligence can be viewed as an acquired characteristic. If the distribution of 'innate' intelligence is random, then the differences in measured intelligence between the social classes may be the outcome of different forms of socialisation. However, it is important to note that differences in the measured intelligence of individuals may be due to differences in 'innate' intelligence (except in the case of identical twins).

Some important reservations should be made about this psycho-cultural model. Intelligence is a social invention. It does not exist in some societies and its origins here can be traced back to the English psychologist Galton, and to Binet and Simon who invented the intelligence test. Acting on the assumption that intelligence was basically genetic, tests were constructed to give a distribution of scores similar to the distribution of biological properties like the length of pea pods; the 'normal curve'. Thus children could be classified and selected using apparently objective scientific methods. The esoteric nature of this knowledge is shown in the way children and their parents are not told their IQ or other scores, and in the restricted sale of the tests used.

In any area where separate forms of secondary education are provided, some kind of selection will be required to decide which primary school pupils go to particular schools. Many local education authorities claim to have abolished the eleven-plus selection test. Unless they have instituted a complete system of non-selective comprehensive schools, this claim usually means that a single test or group of tests is not set at the same time, but the assessment is spread over a period of time, possibly years.

The forms of secondary selection are very variable. As Vernon and others (1957) have shown, almost all selection devices tend to favour middle-class children, that is, they contain an element of *social selection*. The 'brightest' working-class children seem to be the least disadvantaged. The greatest advantage is gained by middle-class borderline candidates. A simple verbal reasoning test seems to have the least disadvantage for working-class children. The use of tricky questions, essays and interviews all favour middle-class pupils. Such pupils are also at an advantage when teachers' assessments are used. As with interviewing, this may be an example of the 'halo effect' in which a single favourable characteristic in the pupil, such as a neat appearance, is taken to indicate a general favourability.

The rate of transfer of pupils between kinds of secondary schools is very low. The few pupils who are transferred from secondary modern schools to grammar schools (usually at thirteen-plus), tend to be middle-class. This could be another example of social selection. It may also reflect the lobbying efforts of articulate middle-class parents in bringing about the transfer (Robbins Report, 1963; App. 1, part 2 contains information about thirteen-plus transfer).

There is a certain irony in the history of ability testing. It was originally introduced in the 1920s, by pioneers such as Burt, as being fairer to working-class children than tests of school work, because performance in the former reflected 'true' ability

23

unaffected by the quality of the home or school (Campbell, 1954). Since the 1950s the demonstration by sociologists and psychologists of the social selection element in their use has led to their being defined as unfair.

Cultural discontinuity theories

The differential income, provision and ability theories are concerned with quantitative differences in the distribution of resources. Cultural discontinuity theories are more qualitative. Basically they all pose that the social classes are subcultural groups with different values, ideas, knowledge, norms of behaviour, speech and even thought forms. Education is regarded as a process of cultural transmission, and it is suggested that the culture transmitted and the means of its transmission are more closely related to the culture of the middle classes that to that of the working classes. Thus children from middle-class backgrounds are regarded as being culturally continuous with the educational process, whereas working-class children may be culturally discontinuous or even experience 'culture clash'.

These theories take different forms and have been applied to a number of social situations including the school, the classroom, the peer group and the family. The first three are dealt with in this chapter, the family in the next. Language, in several connections, is dealt with in chapter 4.

Social class and the experience of school

The main idea behind these studies is that if working-class children do less well than middle-class children this will be reflected in their experience of school. The evidence is mixed.

When secondary school pupils were asked to report their dispositions towards various aspects of school life, King (1973) found there were few consistent differences between pupils from different backgrounds in the same school. Witkin (1974) found no class differences in children's evaluation of English lessons,

24

and suggests that working-class children may actually enjoy some lessons more because the experiences are less familiar to them – a neat inversion of the usual reasoning. Ellison and Williams (1971) found primary school children of all classes preferred the Ladybird reading books to the Nippers series, despite the latter having been written to appeal to working-class children.

However, Case and Ross (1965) found that working-class early leavers showed a strong preference for practical subjects like art and craft. Both the *Early Leaving* report (CAC, 1954) and the Social Survey of the Crowther Report (1960) found that the predominantly working-class early leavers reported unsatisfactory experiences of school, in terms of their relations with teachers and having to wear school uniform, but they regretted the lost educational opportunities in leaving school, and many continued their education part-time at technical colleges. The working- class early leavers in King's (1969) study of a single grammar school showed low levels of involvement in the school in terms of their disposition and participation.

Working-class pupils in most of the thirty secondary schools in another sample studied by King (1973), joined fewer school clubs and had lower expectations for the length of their educational lives compared with middle-class pupils in the same school, suggesting that although the evaluation of school was similar, the working-class children found their experience less relevant to their world outside the school and had less implications for their future.

Overall these studies suggest that it is the less successful working-class children who may have a different kind of experience of school. These usually have fathers with semiskilled or unskilled manual occupations. It may also be the case that middle-class pupils whose experience of school is no more satisfactory may be sustained by their cultural continuity. In the boys' grammar school studied by King (1969), the working-class early leavers from the low streams showed low involvement in the school and had interests and values that were not highly

25

Education

approved by their teachers. Their class mates who stayed on were predominantly middle-class, and were no more involved in the school but held more teacher-approved values.

Teachers' perspectives on their pupils' social class

Some studies give the other side of the school story. The expectation that teachers tend to have poorer evaluations of working-class children is to some extent confirmed. In the National Child Development Survey of the Plowden Report (1967) they were rated by teachers as settling down more slowly in school and as being less amenable to discipline than middle-class infants. Elizabeth Goodacre (1968) found that primary school teachers made perceptions of the social origins of their pupils, and that those of the working class were rather crude stereotypes of inadequate mothers and uncultured homes. She asked the teachers to estimate their pupils' reading ages and found that in the case of the middle-class children there was a good correspondence between the estimates and the reading ages obtained by her testing, but for the working-class children the estimates tended to be lower than the measurements.

This study has sometimes been posed as an example of a *self-fulfilling prophecy*. In Merton's (1957) usage this is 'in the first place a false definition of the situation evoking new behaviour which makes the original false definition come true' (p. 423). The suggestion is that teachers have incorrectly low estimates of working-class children's abilities, and that this leads to their having lower expectations of these children, which in turn leads to their doing less well than they might. This has been called the 'Pygmalion effect' after the ethically dubious experiment in America by Rosenthal and Jacobson (1968), who let teachers have the names of children randomly designated as about the 'bloom' or 'spurt' intellectually. They report that some of these children did improve their intelligence scores, and claim that these gains were the outcome of a self-fulfilling prophecy. However, these results have been disputed, and replications of the experiment have given different results. Most importantly, Rosenthal and Jacobson found that teachers had forgotten the names of most of the spurters, so that it is difficult to understand how they may have changed their behaviour in such a way as to be advantageous to these spurters.

Explanations of social class differences in attainment which pose cultural discontinuity theories have been accused of 'deficit systems thinking' or 'vacuum ideology', the image of the working-class child as lacking the internal social wherewithal to succeed (Keddie, 1973). This 'individuation' of failure has drawn attention away from the part that may be played by teachers and the curriculum. The posing of the self-fulfilling prophecy is therefore attractive to some in putting the blame on the teacher, not the pupil. But the attractiveness of an explanation does not make it correct, and there is little direct evidence to support this one. A basic problem is how the 'real' ability of a child could be established. Furthermore, the evidence of Nash (1973, ch. 2) suggests that teachers use their sometimes false perceptions of their pupils' social origins in order to explain poor behaviour or work, which is in reverse of the requirements for a self-fulfilling prophecy.

Social class and academic streaming

Streaming, the grouping of pupils of the same imputed ability, has also been described as a self-fulfilling prophecy, and one which contributes to the underachievement of working-class children.

It is well established that working-class children are over-represented in bottom streams. This has been shown in primary schools by Douglas (1964) and Jackson (1964), and in secondary schools by Lacey (1970) and Holly (1965). However, it would be wrong to assume that this distribution of the social classes always occurs. In a survey of different kinds of secondary school, King (1973) found the over-representation of working-class pupils in the bottom streams in a quarter of the second years and a third of the fourth years, but not one example of the over-representation of middle-class pupils.

This distribution between the streams is the outcome of the allocation processes used, which vary from the use of 'objective' tests to teachers' subjective impressions. These processes may include an element of social selection, perhaps sometimes another example of the halo effect in which a single approved characteristic, such as a 'nice' way of talking, is generalised to assumptions of overall suitability. Lacey (1970) found that some middle-class parents in the grammar school he studied actually lobbied the teachers to ensure their sons entered the top stream.

It is very well established that pupils in the low streams show a lower level of involvement in school than those in the higher streams. This has been measured using teachers' estimates of pupils' dispositions, pupils' self-reported dispositions towards many aspects of school, their self-reported behaviour, and by direct observations, in studies by Jackson (1964) and Lunn (1970) in primary schools, Hargreaves (1967) Lacey (1970) and King (1973) in secondary schools. Once again it would be wrong to assume that low stream always goes with low involvement. It occurred in about half of the sample of secondary schools studied by King; it was more common in grammar schools and among boys in both single and mixed sex schools.

Not surprisingly, it is also well established that low stream pupils do less well in school work than those in high streams. Dale and Griffiths (1965) study of a Welsh grammar school describes the phenomenon of stream slipping, where children demoted from higher streams slip down to the bottom to become the core of mainly working-class early leavers. In general the rate of transfer between streams is usually small, with more promotion than demotion.

Another element is the teacher. Both Hargreaves (1967) and Lacey (1970), in their closely related studies, found the teachers held strong stereotypes of the 'bright' A stream and the 'thick' bottom stream. Jackson (1969) has suggested that in primary schools the 'bright' lively teachers are assigned to top streams,

28

and the 'dull plodders' to the bottom. Lacey found that the heads of academic departments commonly taught the top streams (1970). In another case study King (1969) showed that boys were well aware of the view their teachers took of the stream system.

These then are the elements (except one) of the supposed self-fulfilling prophecy of streaming. Streaming labels children according to their supposed capacity for school work. Teachers relate to children according to their stream status in ways that lead to those in top streams doing well at school work and those in bottom streams doing poorly. Since bottom streams tend to be disproportionately working-class in composition, streaming contributes to social class differences in attainment.

How acceptable is this analysis? First, the missing element. In Merton's definition the self-fulfilling prophecy begins with a false definition. Are children's abilities falsely defined when they are allocated to streams? In twenty-one secondary schools using streaming in the second year, nineteen showed the expected higher mean scores for intelligence in the top streams (the two exceptions were grammar schools with narrow ability ranges: (King, 1973). If the reservations made about the measurement of intelligence are laid aside, it is to be expected that working-class children would be over-represented in bottom streams because of the relationship between social class and measured intelligence already indicated. Douglas claimed that at the borderline of measured ability between streams middle-class children were more commonly allocated to top streams, a social selection similar to the borderline cases in the eleven-plus (Douglas, 1964). This evidence should be treated cautiously because the 491 children in Douglas's sample came from 491 different schools, so that the group of borderliners considered in the analysis had no actual social existence in a school or schools, and no one actually chose pupils from this group for allocation to streams. Statistical groups should reflect social groups.

These same reservations apply to Douglas's measurements of ability in relation to streaming. Between the ages of eight and eleven the less able in the top stream tended to improve their test scores, especially the middle-class pupils, while the more able in the bottom stream tended to do less well, especially the working-class pupils. This may look like the self-fulfilling prophecy confirmed but these results may be statistical artifacts due to the artificial nature of the two 'streams' each consisting of over 200 children from different schools who were never actually taught together. In addition the work of Horobin (1967) suggests that the apparent opening up of the 'class gap' between the streams over the three-year period would be expected from the kinds of ability tests used.

A test of the 'effects' of streaming could be made by a comparison with non-streaming or mixed ability groups. Lunn (1970) attempted to do this for primary schools and concluded that overall there were few differences in the levels of attainment and disposition towards school in the different forms of grouping, although there were advantages for boys of low ability in non--streamed classes. These results should be treated cautiously since she drew samples of children from seventy-two different schools, and then compared the scores for all children from all the streamed schools with all children from all the non-streamed schools. Neither of these groups had an actual social existence so that the reported differences (or lack of them) could again be statistical artifacts.

There are undoubtedly variations in pupil–teacher relationships between streams which may have significant consequences for learning, but on the basis of the available evidence it cannot be definitely concluded that streaming acts as a self-fulfilling prophecy accounting for the relative failure of working-class children. As with the previous discussion of teacher–pupil relations the problem is to define 'real' ability.

Streaming is probably better seen in terms of W. I. Thomas's (1928) *definition of the situation* 'If men define situations as real they are real in their consequences'. In secondary schools King (1973) found that what children were taught and how they were assessed often varied by stream. When low stream pupils are judged incapable of learning French they are taught no French, so that none may be entered for exams in French, so that the original definition is never tested and is therefore assumed to be true or real.

(Other aspects of streaming are dealt with in chapter 5.)

Social class, values and knowledge

Several studies have been based on the assumption that educational success depends on the possession or acceptance of values as kinds of choices, and forms of thought that are characteristically middle- rather than working-class.

Sugarman (1966), in a study of fourth-year boys in four secondary schools, followed the theories of Kluckhohn and Strodtbeck in testing their value orientations towards time, activity and social relationships, the proposition being that educational success would be associated with the supposed middle-class values of an orientation towards the future, a stress on activity in relation to success, and individuality. He found that boys who did well in school work and were judged well-behaved did tend to make these kinds of choices, irrespective of their social class of origin. Working-class boys who were not judged so favourably tended to make what were thought to be more characteristically working-class choices; a present orientation (having a good time now), a stress on being (an acceptance of the prevailing situation) and collaterality (sticking with your mates).

Some of these ideas are also found in Hargreaves's (1967) study of secondary modern school boys, where he uses Weber's concept of the Protestant ethic, which is assumed to be more middle- than working-class. Using pupils' answers to questions, their self reported behaviour, observations and teachers ratings he found that the 'successful' pupils more often showed the following characteristics:

1. Ambition regarded as a virtue.
2. Individual responsibility, resourcefulness and self-reliance.
3. Cultivation and possession of skills.

4. Worldly asceticism, postponement of immediate satisfaction in the interest of long-term achievement.
5. Rationality and planning.
6. Cultivation of manners, courtesy and personality.
7. Control of physical aggression and violence.
8. Wholesome recreation.
9. Respect for property.

Nell Keddie's (1971) research in the teaching of social studies in a secondary school was based mainly on observations and interviews. In her analysis of the teaching of a topic on the family she suggests that pupils regarded as less able (mainly working-class) preferred to keep to their own 'commonsense' knowledge rather than accept their teacher's 'expert' knowledge. Good pupils (mainly middle-class) accepted the 'objectified' view of the family they were taught.

Friendships, social class and attainment

One aspect of friendships in relation to education has been illustrated in a preceding section. Compared with their relationships with teachers, their encounter with school and their parents (to be dealt with in the next chapter) friends are probably less important in a pupil's educational career. However, for some working-class pupils they may be quite important. Halsey and Gardner (1953) showed that grammar school boys formed friendships according to how well they were doing in their work, irrespective of social class of origins. Thus some working-class children's efforts and ambitions may be sustained by contact with middle-class friends. The other side of the situation is shown in the *Early Leaving* report's (CAC, 1954) finding that the mainly working-class early leavers often had friends out at work and may have felt tempted to leave early in order to have the same buying power.

The relationship between friendship group and academic progress is a classic chicken–egg problem: which came first? Does work deteriorate when someone falls in with a bad lot, or vice versa?

The family and education 3

The power of parents to decide the life-chances of their children has been greatly reduced. Laws have been introduced to prevent their beating, starving and otherwise ill-treating their own children. Other laws prevent children from going to work and make education compulsory, although parents still have the power of decision about education after sixteen (Fletcher, 1966; Musgrove, 1966).

Human beings have to learn to be human. There are fairly well authenticated cases of children who were reared by wild animals, such as wolves, and who acquired the behavioural characteristics of the animals that fostered them. The cultural differences between societies are associated with different kinds of child-rearing processes, that is, differences in early socialisation. It is not surprising to find that class subcultures are also associated with different patterns of child-rearing. Middle-class children may be socialised in such a way as to take greater advantage of formal education than working-class children. The class differences in attainment discussed in the last chapter were presented in terms of fathers' occupational groups. These occupational groupings may be seen as crude representations of different kinds of families.

The critical question is, which aspects of middle-class families create educational advantages? The related question exists, which aspects of working-class families create educational disadvantages? Psychological answers to these questions have stressed events in early childhood, including weaning and pot-training. However, there have been fashions in the popularity of early and late weaning and pot-training among middle-class mothers in the last forty years, but there have been no accompanying fluctuations in the rate of educational attainment among middle-class children (Bronfenbrenner, 1958). (The working-class wife is likely to turn to her mother for advice about problems with her children; the middle-class wife turns to her child care manual written by experts.)

The contribution of the family to educability is clearly a complex one. The suggestion is that although the power of parents in this respect has declined, their influence has increased (Musgrove, 1966).

Social class differences in child-rearing

The husband and wife team of John and Elizabeth Newson have spent most of their professional lives conducting a longitudinal study of parents and their children in Nottingham, based mainly on detailed interviews with the mothers (Newson and Newson, 1963, 1970, 1976). Their work has revealed hundreds of differences in family life among the social classes. In reporting some of them, which may have educational relevance, the terms middle class and working class will be used. In general what is being referred to is a gradient in the frequency from the professional classes to the unskilled manual class.

Middle-class mothers are less likely to smack their children, or to threaten them with authority figures such as policemen, or to threaten to send them away or withdraw their love. They emphasise table manners more than working-class mothers and stick to regular bedtimes. They play with their children more often in a designated indoor play space, and arbitrate in their quarrels. Middle-class children more often have bedtime stories read to them, and their mothers are more likely to tell them where babies come from rather than to give gooseberry bush explanations. Their occasional rudeness, tantrums and bad language tend to be ignored.

Among seven-year-olds, working-class children are more likely to be allowed to play out or roam the streets without having told their parents where or with whom they are going. They tend to be given more pocket money than middle-class seven-year-olds but they receive it less regularly and are less likely to be encouraged to save some of it. The Newsons have pointed out that the physical aspects of housing provision can have important consequences. The mother in an owner-occupied house with its own garden can observe and mediate in the activities of her children and their invited friends from the kitchen window. The garden gate defines a social world. The children of back-to-back houses with only small yards play in the street, largely unobserved by their mothers, but subject to the admonitions of any adult in the road ('Go and play somewhere else').

Other studies have suggested that middle-class husbands are more likely to share in household matters with their wives, and this sharing of conjugal roles is shown in the higher participation of middle-class fathers in the upbringing of their children. Overall, the Newsons find that middle-class households are more child-centred, and that middle-class parents while generating more rules and principles regarding their children's behavioural relationships with others, tend to make their basis clearer, so implying their universal nature, but they also allow for individual differences and lapses on the child's part. Working-class children tend to be freer of parental supervision but when they are rewarded or disciplined it tends to reflect their parents' disposition more than their own actions.

The fourth as yet unpublished volume of the Newsons' work concerns the seven-year-olds in school. However, it is already possible at least to glimpse some of the elements of middle-class family life associated with educational success.

Social class and family size

Middle-class families tend to be smaller in size than working-class ones, and the children tend to be more widely spaced.

Table 3.1 *Social class and family size*

Father's occupation	Mean family size	
	1951	1961
Professional and managerial	1.9	1.7
Clerical	2.0	1.6
Skilled manual	2.4	1.9
Semiskilled manual	2.8	2.0
Unskilled manual	3.2	2.4

Source. Derived from the 1951 and 1961 Census Fertility Tables.

The mean family size has fallen over a period of 100 years, mainly due to the use of birth control, but a social class differential has remained.

Middle-class children tend to have a higher measured intelligence and a longer educational life than working-class children (chapter 2). The mean scores for measured intelligence are higher in smaller families than larger ones. Are social class differences in education therefore explained by differences in family size? The evidence of the Crowther Report (1960) and Douglas (1964) suggest that coming from a small family seems to be most advantageous to working-class pupils. This may sometimes be an economic matter; the family income can support the extended education of one or two children, but not more.

Parents' attitudes to education

The large-scale surveys of parents by Douglas (1964) and that commissioned by the Plowden Committee (1967) show that middle-class parents profess a greater educational ambition for their children and report a greater interest in their education, including visiting the school and talking to the teachers. It should be stressed that although working-class parents report less interest in their children's education, there is no evidence to suggest they are generally less interested in their children. For example, the Plowden survey showed no class differences in the frequency with which mothers attend the medical examination of their children.

There is a statistical relationship between parents' self-reported interest in their children's education and how well the children do at school. The Plowden Committee assumed that this positive correlation was a causal connection; that high parental interest lead to high levels of success. This was in line with their recommendation that there should be an increase in parental involvement in education through parent–teacher associations. Furthermore, it followed that if the attitudes of working-class parents could be 'improved' the class gap in educational attainment would be reduced.

There is however no evidence of such a causal connection. Young and McGeeny (1968) found no significant increase in junior school pupils' attainment when their parents' interest was increased. Douglas (1964) showed that parents whose children were demoted from A to B streams tended to reduce their interest and ambitions for their child. Here the level of educational success may be influencing parents, rather than the other way around. As Bernstein and Davies (1969) have pointed out the Plowden Report's calculation of the relative 'effects' of parents' attitudes (high) and schools (low) on attainment was suspect on the grounds of its assumptions and the data used. There is sometimes a big gap between what parents express attitudes and how they behave with their children.

Of greater significance are the studies forming part of a research programme under the direction of Basil Bernstein (see reference list, p. 154). Working-class mothers tended to consider that the purpose of play was to keep children amused and 'out of the way'. Middle-class mothers placed greater emphasis on the value of toys and play in providing new and wider experiences for the child, in a way similar to the controlled-play atmosphere of the infant class. Furthermore, middle-class mothers often took active steps to prepare their children for school, smoothing the introduction process by taking them to visit the school before they officially started, making introductions to their teacher-to-be, and showing where the lavatories were. They tend to be prepared for an active pupil role and encouraged to take part in things and ask questions. Working-class mothers were less likely to prepare their children for school in this way. Working-class children were more often prepared for a passive pupil role. Mothers stressed the need to be well behaved, to keep out of mischief and be quiet and attentive. The prospect of school may be presented through phrases like, 'You won't be able to do that when you go to school'.

These are indications that middle-class families tend to be in better cultural continuity with the school than working class families.

Family life and education

Studies of communities in Britain often use families as the units in the analysis. From these studies, many of them collated by Josephine Klein (1965), it is possible to suggest the existence of several types of family, to which actual families will correspond by varying degrees. As there is an element of class voyeurism in these studies far more is known about working-class areas and families than middle-class ones.

Middle-class parents are likely to have more knowledge and experience of education than working-class parents (Floud, 1954). Swift (1968) has suggested that established or *second generation middle-class families* tend to place an intrinsic value on education: extended education is something that people in their position have, a symbol as much as a prerequisite of their status, a symbol often bought by private education. In *first generation middle-class families* the evaluation of education tends to be more in terms of occupational opportunities. Where a father has gained lower middle-class status by career mobility, often through the foreman position, Swift suggests that his 'mobility pessimism', the realisation he can advance no further without more qualifications, may lead to his visiting his ambitions on his son. Such boys were advantaged in the eleven-plus examination.

Some working-class parents may have just as good an understanding and acceptance of the educational system as many middle-class parents. This may be the case where a wife has 'married down', where she may have had a superior education or occupation to her husband – the D. H. Lawrence syndrome. In addition there are *sunken middle-class families*; a result of downward social mobility. The grandparents may be middle-class but the parents working-class by occupational classification. Jackson and Marsden (1962) suggest that many successful grammar school pupils come from such atypical working-class homes.

Other working-class parents may have high hopes for their children but may not have much personal experience of the kind of education they wish for their children. These are likely to be *aspiring working-class* families, anxious for their children to improve themselves socially by entering middle-class occupations through success in the exam system. One kind of aspiring working-class family is the *traditional–respectable*. They feel themselves to be better than most others in the street, they are status dissenters forming what Jackson and Marsden (1962) call 'small enclaves of respectability'. The family is likely to be a small one whose unity is emphasised by common activities, often associated with a church or political organisation. The father is likely to have a skilled or semiskilled job and mother stays at home; their conjugal roles are shared. There may be an emphasis on politeness and cooperation within these families; the children are often educational successes.

The later 1950s saw the emergence of what Ferdinand Zweig (1961) called 'the newly affluent' workers. These were the skilled and semiskilled manual workers who began to earn high wages in industries manufacturing consumer goods. The studies of Goldthorpe and Lockwood (Goldthorpe *et al*, 1967) of a sample of such workers in the car industry in Luton found that relative affluence had not led to their becoming middle-class in their life-styles, even though some had bought their own houses, but they had become more home centred. Zweig had been struck by the sight of working-class fathers pushing prams – something unthinkable twenty years before.

Newly affluent families are likely to be small, and the mother may supplement the family income by taking a part-time job once the children have started school. (There is no evidence that children are educationally disadvantaged by their mothers going to work; there are many teacher-mothers: Frazer, 1973.) The family emphasises material possessions. Their furniture is new and well kept, the home bright and freshly decorated. Family unity is emphasised by watching television together, and by weekend trips in the family car. These parents want their children to have 'the best of everything' and that includes education. Toomey (1970), in a study of workers in a Medway town, found that the children of such affluent home-centred families had a longer educational life than those from less affluent families.

Other working-class parents may take a delegative view of education. Their attitude in bringing their child to school is 'take him and do what you like with him'. This is the *solid working-class* kind of family, large, rather easygoing, taking life as it comes. The father, usually with a semiskilled or unskilled job, is the nominal head of the family. In stereotype, he has his own chair, has his meals served first, and drinks tea from a bigger cup than anyone else. He reserves a proportion of his wages for his own amusement, which he may take apart from the rest of the family at the pub or club. The home is mother-centred. She is not likely to go out to work; she and her husband agree that her place is in the home. She manages the family budget but may never know how much her husband actually earns. The relationships in these families may seem casual, but they generate strong emotional bonds that make family values hard to betray, and it is possible that doing well at school and 'getting on' may constitute such a betrayal. Young and Willmott (1960) reported that grammar school places were not taken up in

Bethnel Green for fear of 'going above our station'; status assenting.

Other working-class parents may also be delegative in their attitude towards education, but sometimes even hostile towards teachers and possessive about their children. This is the *rough or deprived family*. Here the father is a poorly paid, usually unskilled worker, often in-and-out of work rather than unemployed. The family is large and tends to have poor quality housing, and to live in what to middle-class eyes seems like untidiness, even squalor, which they seem unable or unwilling to cope with. The home provides little privacy. The parents have little care for social conventions. Mother and father follow almost separate lives; the children are alternately neglected and indulged. This kind of family regards life as a matter of luck. They spend their money quickly for a good time, by gambling and buying luxuries rather than necessities, and although the mother may take a succession of part-time jobs, the money often runs out midweek.

There are two important concluding points to be made about the family and education which arise from this typology. Firstly, it is a corrective to the rather crude, oversimplified view of the middle-class family and the working-class family. There are many different kinds of families. There is evidence of variation by region and it is likely that some kinds of family life are strongly related to the nature of the father's occupation. The studies of fishermen, lorry drivers and shift workers show how their work affects their relationships with their wives and children. There is scope for some research into the family lives of teachers; the high incidence of endogamy means that many children may have two teachers as parents.

Much of the early research on the family was centred on the idea of a model family, the *educogenic family*, one with all the characteristics to ensure the educational success of the children (Floud, 1961, 1970; Musgrove, 1966). The second important point is that the evidence strongly suggests that children who do well in school may come from a number of different kinds of family, and what may be advantageous in one situation may not

41

be in another. Finally, as one corrective to the notion that educational success is 'determined' by the family, it should be pointed out that against the odds some children from 'good' homes do fail, whilst others from 'bad' ones succeed.

Language and education 4

Language is a part of the culture of a society. It is also the most important medium for the transmission of that culture, within both the family and the educational system. Not only is it the major medium for the transmission of facts and skills, but many of our values, beliefs, norms and roles are learnt through language. The intimate relationship between culture and language is illustrated by the studies of non-literate societies, where the lexicon (the use of words) and syntax (the arrangement of words) reflect aspects of culture and social structure. For example, specific names may be given to family relationships which are not named in our society, indicating their greater importance.

In modern industrialised societies there exist a plurality of social groups, some of which may be considered to be subcultures with distinctive speech or even language patterns. This is clear in the case of Belgium with its French and Flemish language groups. In this country social distinctions are made on the basis of dialects, which are mainly regional, and accent, which may also be regional but also have social class connotations. One of the stereotypes of the 'educated' person is the use of an 'Oxford' or 'BBC' accent. This 'received pronunciation' has been propagated through the public schools and their imitators, as well as by elocution teachers drawing their clients from the children of the socially aspiring. Regional accents generally have 'uneducated' and working-class connotations, although these are less clear than they used to be (Trugill, 1974).

The work of Basil Bernstein is not concerned with dialect or accent but with the structure of language and its use in social contexts and relationships, particularly in education and the family. There are many problems involved in attempting to give a short account of this important work. Its scale is one (see Bernstein, p. 156). Bernstein's earliest paper was published in 1958 and the complete bibliography of the publications by him and his associates is very long, and there are still more planned. His early, modest, small-scale research was developed into one of the largest and most ambitious projects in British sociology, creating a mass of data and results. His theories have formed the basis of the research but these have been continually extended and modified to take into account the research results, so that at what appears to be the terminal stage of the work the latest most complex theoretical perspectives are unlikely to be tested (Bernstein, 1971). Finally, in attempting to express complex and difficult ideas Bernstein's writings are also often difficult and complex. The presentation made here will therefore of necessity be something of a simplification. The version of his *sociolinguistic theory of social learning* will be one that uses the most simple linguistic terms, and which has been most tested by the research.

Bernstein's sociolinguistic theory of social learning

The neglect of language by sociologists meant that the early work drew upon other disciplines; from psychology the work of the Russians Luria and Vygotsky, from anthropology the work of Sapir and Whorf, and from linguistics that of Halliday and Goldman–Eisler (Lawton, 1970). But the basis of his concern was the growing evidence of social class differences in educational attainment.

When language is regarded as a code with a lexical and syntactic structure used for sending speech messages, the nature of the code is seen to reflect aspects of the social structure and culture of the society in which it is used. From this Bernstein made his imaginative leap. If language codes differ from one culture to another then it is possible that the social class subcultural differences within British society may be associated with different codes. He proposed the existence of two kinds of codes: one group with similar structural characteristics are called *restricted codes*; the other is the *elaborated code*. The codes not only differ in structure but also in function. This is because the nature of the message transmitted is related to the structure of the code used to transmit it.

The structure and functions of restricted codes

All adults are able to use a number of restricted codes. Some of them are societal in that virtually all members of British society use them. These are used, for example, in conversations about the weather and when people meet each other, especially for the first time. Other restricted codes are more specific. They are used in small groups such as families, among friends, in army units, prisons, work teams and localities. Each occupational group tends to generate its own restricted code, a part of 'shop talk'.

These codes function mainly to reinforce existing relationships and confirm understandings. They are usually used between people who know one another and may have similar social characteristics. When used among unequals they are associated with *positional authority relationships,* which are well defined and fairly independent of the individuals concerned, for example, a sergeant major with troops on the parade ground. These speech codes are *context bound* in that their meanings only make sense in a given social setting. The codes may be used to exclude outsiders and remote cohesion within the group. In general terms 'the ability to switch codes is the ability to switch roles'. The more codes available to an individual the greater the number of roles that are also available.

Bernstein suggests that working-class people tend to be confined to the use of restricted codes, mainly ones related to their social positions and occupations, and have only limited access to the elaborated code. More specifically he suggests that the unskilled manual workers and their families are almost entirely confined to the use of restricted codes; that is, about 10 per cent of the population.

The structure of restricted codes reflects their functions. The important structural features are suggested to be as follows:

(a) The syntax is simple and rigid, there are few subordinate clauses. The short simple sentences are often left unfinished.
(b) Few adverbs and adjectives are used and they are of limited range.
(c) The verbal form stresses the active mood.
(d) The speaker may choose from a group of idiomatic phrases, e.g. 'hello', 'how do you do', 'pleased to meet you', 'watcher'.
(e) There are a few pauses, and gaps in the flow may be filled with phrases that have no particular meaning but serve to promote what was originally called 'sympathetic circularity', e.g. 'you know', 'you see'.
(f) The meaning of the message relayed by the code is generally implicit. The literal meaning of a phrase may be nonsense but its implied meaning is clear, e.g. 'get knotted' (my example).
(g) Nuances of meaning are made by the tone of the voice, by facial expressions, the attitude of the body and other non-verbal signs, such as bodily contact. For example the phrase 'watch it mate' (my example) has an implied general meaning something like, 'pay careful regard to your behaviour in this situation'. It may be used to give some timely advice to a friend. The same phrase said with a different tone of voice and accompanied by quite different non-verbal signals, e.g. staring eyes and pointing finger, may act as a serious warning to a potential adversary.

The structure and functions of the elaborated code

The use of the elaborated code is associated more with middle-class, non-manual occupational groups. Although it may be used sometimes to initiate relationships it is used mainly to communicate ideas, precise information, and the accurate description of processes. The meanings of messages conveyed through the code may be understood without other information; it is *context free*. Its use is associated with *personal authority*, independent of office and dependent on individual negotiation. Its suggested structure reflects these functions.

(a) The structure is complex and includes many subordinate clauses.
(b) Many varied adjectives and adverbs are used.
(c) The verbal form tends to stress the passive mood.
(d) The construction of phrases is made by the speaker transmitting the message.
(e) There are frequent pauses.
(f) The meanings transmitted are explicit and nuances are expressed verbally. The speaker does not orientate his transmission of the code to the listener as in the restricted code, but to the content of the message he wishes to convey. The meaning of spoken elaborated code is clear when it is reproduced in writing (e.g. the transcript of a lecture). This is not necessarily so for restricted codes.

The educational implications of the theory

The postulated elaborated code would be the basis of many speech acts in education: the teacher in introducing ideas, facts and procedures, and the pupils in reproducing these in the assessment of having learnt and understood them. The language of school books is structurally similar to the elaborated code; as is that used in essays and other written exercises. If middle-class children come to school with the ability to use the elaborated code they are therefore at an advantage over working-class children who have less access to this code, and may have to learn it, almost as a prelude to formal learning. Hence differential access to the elaborated code forms an explanation of social class differences in educational attainment.

Similarly, intelligence and other selection tests have a high verbal loading, and the language used is similar to the postulated elaborated code. Such tests are therefore not entirely culturally neutral; they are substantially middle class. In particular this refers to the verbal structure of the test rather than its content, that is, *how* a question is asked rather than *what* question is asked, although the two may be related. Only certain kinds of question can be asked using a particular language. Verbal measured intelligence may be regarded as a middle-class characteristic, and hence its variation between the social classes. Measurements of non-verbal intelligence show little or no social class variation.

Children are not born with the use of language; it is acquired through interaction with adults, particularly the mother. The posed differences in access to the elaborated code among children from different backgrounds must therefore be attributed to social class differences in the use of language in the child rearing process; essentially the mother–child relationship.

The sociolinguistic theory of codes is therefore one of the most sophisticated versions of the cultural discontinuity theory of social class differences in educational attainment. The next sections look at the research and the evidence to support the theory.

Children's language

Bernstein's early work used post office messenger boys on day-release courses and public school boys as subjects, eliciting speech samples in interviews, analysing their written work and measuring their verbal and non-verbal ability quotients. Lawton (1968) replicated some of these approaches with a tighter research design. The main research programme started in 1962 with the setting up of the Sociological Research Unit at the London Institute of Education. The subjects were about 450 children, their mothers and their teachers from two contrasted areas, one a working-class, the other a middle-class suburb. The children were rising five years old, about to start infant schooling when they were first investigated, and the studies continued until they were over seven.

Many methods were used to obtain samples of children's speech representing a range of tasks. For example, descriptive and narrative speech were elicited by the use of a model room, picture story and other cards, explanatory speech by asking children to say how games were played, and showing them a wind-up toy elephant that went through a series of sequential movements. Analysis of these samples showed middle-class children tended to use more verbs, nouns, adverbs and adjectives than working-class children of the same sex and measured intelligence. Middle-class children are claimed to show greater linguistic flexibility in moving from a descriptive to a narrative or explanatory speech task. Their speech is said to be less context bound than that of working-class children. The stories they tell in interpreting a series of pictures can more often be understood independently of the pictures. Working-class children in describing how to play hide-and-seek more often do so using particular children and locations. (Bernstein, *ed.*, 1972; Brandis and Henderson, 1970.)

The results show a great many social class differences in the children's use of language, but nowhere in the results is an example of either an elaborated or restricted code reported. Robinson (1972), a co-worker of Bernstein, claims, however, that the results are consistent with the existence of such codes and with the postulate of the greater access of middle-class children to the elaborated code. An analogy would be with gravity; we can only demonstrate its existence by its effects.

The speech samples were obtained in test situations by trained research workers. Although in many cases the tasks were very similar to those that infant teachers set for individual children, criticisms have been made of the unnatural experimental social context. The linguist Labov reports that formal interviews with black American youths give an impression of inarticulateness, but on their own ground, sitting on the floor with the interviewer,

Education

they were more loquatious, especially when encouraged to use obscenities (Keddie, ed., 1973; Labov, 1972). Labov's criticisms are based upon a limited reading and misinterpretation of Bernstein's works, who is incorrectly accused of stating that the restricted code is inferior to the elaborated, and that the working classes are inarticulate and incapable of logical thought. Labov's own illustrations, using interviews with working-class Larry and middle-class educated Charles (both blacks), are somewhat loaded and rather unconvincing. Labov has to use what Bernstein's theory would call an elaborated code to explain the logic of Larry's conversation.

Bernstein's own view of the connection between speech and thought forms has been discussed in relation to the so-called Whorfian hypothesis. 'We cut up nature – organise it into concepts – and ascribe significances as we do largely because of the absolute obligatory patterns of our language' (Lawton, 1968). Labov assumes that Bernstein accepts the linguistic determination of this hypothesis; put simply, speech expresses thought. However, in his later work Bernstein has withdrawn from the obvious implication of this view, which is, if children of different classes use language differently then they must use different thought forms, and since working-class children do less well at school they must have a limited capacity to use the forms of thought appropriate to educational tasks. Coulthard (1969) has pointed out that Bernstein's theories operate at three levels, the linguistic, the social and the psychological. The extensive linguistic analysis has revealed important social aspects of the use of language (particularly in the child rearing process to be dealt with in the next section), but has not necessarily uncovered the psychological processes of understanding.

The criticism about the methods of obtaining speech samples is an important one and is also made by Rosen (1972). Two points should be made about this. Firstly an attempt was made to record children's speech in 'real life' situations in school using radio transmitters, but these were technological failures. Secondly, given the nature of the research design and the statistical analysis, it was necessary to have certain controls, for example, giving the same speech task to every child.

Language and child-rearing

Two aspects of this work, the mothers' preparation of their children for school and their perceptions of the uses of toys, were mentioned in the last chapter. These and the other studies of the child-rearing process were not based on observations or recordings of mothers with their children, and therefore do not relate to 'real life' situations. There are enormous problems in trying to do this and the results would be very difficult to quantify.

Robinson and Rackstraw (1972) asked mothers of five-year-olds to give the answers they would give if their children had asked particular questions such as, 'Why does daddy shave?', and, 'Why do leaves fall off the trees?'. Working-class mothers' self-reported answers were often not answers at all. For example, to the question about leaf-fall, 'Why shouldn't they?' or, 'Because they do'. Middle-class mothers more often reported longer answers with some attempt at an explanation, for example, 'Leaves are alive and all living things die'. When the children were seven they were asked to answer the same questions, and Robinson and Rackstraw claim that there is some resemblance between the kind of answers they gave and those their mothers said they would have given to them two years previously.

Other self-reported use of language by mothers in relation to their children was used to construct a maternal communication index score. High scores indicating much use of language were associated with middle-class mothers. Working-class mothers reported use of language stressed skills such as children dressing themselves; the middle class stress the use of language in dealing with people in social situations (some of this appears in Brandis and Henderson, 1970).

Mothers and their seven-year-old children were asked related questions by Jenny Cook-Gumperz (1973). In a complex analysis involving the answers to six questions the results suggest that middle-class mothers use more personal control of their children using such strategies as diversions and anticipatory avoidance in relation to behaviour problems. Working-class mothers use more imperative control based upon their position as mothers. These include threats, commands and physical punishments.

These results, which resemble those of the Newson's surveys mentioned in the last chapter, suggest important social class differences in mother-child relations mediated through language, which may also be a means of the cultural reproduction of forms of social relationships and orientations towards the social world.

Mothers, children's language and education

The many strands of this extensive and complex research are difficult to pull together. Most of the many measurements made of the language usage of mothers and their children have been statistically correlated together with their other characteristics. With great simplification they show that these variables go together in a fairly predictable way (Brandis and Henderson, 1970). High social class of mother is associated with the use of language related to the hypothesised elaborated code, both of which are associated with the extensive use of language to control their children and their cultural continuity with the school in terms of such things as the active preparation of children for school. Many of these variables are associated with children's use of language resembling the hypothesised elaborated code and with high IQ measurements. This complexity of correlations gives the impression of massive middle-class advantage. However the working-class mothers of children with high IQs shared many of the same language and child-rearing characteristics of the middle-class mothers, suggesting the possibility that these characteristics may be important to a child's school performance independently of class.

The intervention experiment

These ideas are also implicit in the experiment carried out by the husband and wife team of the Gahagans (1970). Three of the nine schools in a working-class area were the experimental schools in which the teachers, in consultation with the researchers, introduced a programme of language intervention or talk reform. For twenty minutes each day children followed activities designed to encourage the use of language in different contexts. These were developed from some already in use by teachers and were kept deliberately cheap and simple. They included the O'Grady game, listening in the dark, silly sentences, listening to recorded stories, the use of telephones, I-spy and group discussions. In three other control schools matched children were tested over the same period of time, as were those in the three Hawthorne control schools where, knowing from the famous Hawthorne studies that people may change their behaviour when studied, the teachers were given just as much attention as those in the experimental schools and were encouraged to develop projects of their own choosing.

After three years it was found that there were fewer low scorers on verbal intelligence tests among the children in the experimental school, but girls benefited more than boys. These modest results have to be set against the modest nature of the intervention programme. Bernstein has in retrospect regretted that it was carried out before the adequate testing of the theory behind it.

Schools as organisations   5

Schools, together with colleges and universities, are the legally established organisations of the educational process. Some of the activities that go on in schools have the sanction of law. Children up to sixteen must receive full-time education. They must receive religious education and, unless specifically exempt, attend school assembly. Other activities are externally controlled through the Department of Education and Science (DES), such as the provision of milk and meals, and through the local education authority (LEA), including the conditions of the teachers' employment, as well as the examination agencies of the universities and CSE boards. But, much of what goes on in schools is not clearly prescribed, and is decided by the head-teacher and teachers. Their autonomy is not without its constraints. Teachers are subordinate to the head-teachers, and both require the legitimation and compliance of their pupils and their parents (see chapter 1). In addition, many activities are traditionally expected and form part of the British idea of the school. (Aspects of the organisation of particular kinds of school are dealt with in chapters 5 and 6.)

The ideology of the school as a community

The concept of the school held in this country is that it is or should be a community with unique features, concerned not only with the transmission of basic skills and facts (instrumental activities in Bernstein's usage – chapter 1), but also with the transmission of beliefs, values and models of behaviour (expressive activities) – what may be called 'character training' or 'personality development'. This set of ideas, or ideology, may be used to explain and justify many activities, including the school assembly, school uniform, the pastoral care system and prefects; all traditional aspects of British schools (King, 1976). This *ideology of the school as a community* also has strong implications for what it is to be a head-teacher, teacher or pupil. (For a full discussion see chapter 9).

The origin of the idea of the school as a community, and of the expressive activities associated with it, is in the public schools of the nineteenth century. The ancient foundation schools had been strongly criticised during the Napoleonic wars for their narrow curriculum and poor teaching, but much concern was expressed about the delinquent behaviour of their upper-middle-class pupils, leading on several occasions to rebellions, as at Winchester in 1808, which was only ended by the intervention of the militia with bayonets (Mack, 1938).

The structural reforms particularly associated with Thomas Arnold of Rugby were mainly intended to assert social control and obtain order. The private boarding houses were incorporated into the schools and formed the basis of the House system. Secular and sacred authority were fused in the elevation of chapel attendance as a major element of school life. The new schools, established later to meet the demands made by the newly emergent middle classes for a gentleman's education for their sons, were built in rural areas, not only for economic reasons but also to isolate the pupils from the temptations of town. These and other changes cohered round the idea of the school as a community.

As with many successful innovations these became institutionalised and came to be regarded as being intrinsically worthwhile. Measures taken to establish control were valued not only as a means to this end, but also as ends in themselves. The social isolation of the schools as communities of men and boys with similar social origins, the tight organisation of all pupil activities and the emphasis on conformity, both formal and informal, were justified in terms of their generating the character qualities required in the pupils' eventual careers as army officers and senior civil servants, often in the outposts of the Empire. 'The educational community [was made] a symbol for other communities which would claim the individual's loyalty' (Wilkinson, 1963).

These ideas about the nature of the school and education were adopted by the new grammar schools set up by the local authorities after the 1902 Education Act. This followed from the general acceptance of the public schools as an appropriate model (Banks, 1955). Since then their origins have become largely forgotten, they have become institutionalised, receiving the legitimacy of tradition, largely unconsidered and taken for granted. However, for teachers and especially head-teachers the ideology of the school as a community has a greater importance because it is the source of legitimacy for many of their actions and also is bound up with their identities. In interviews with head-teachers and in the analysis of documents written by them or produced with their approval, King (1973) found frequent references to the school as a community, such as, 'we aim to be a happy, well-ordered community'.

The idea that each school community should possess individuality and a measure of independence is used to legitimise the considerable autonomy of head-teachers; power to achieve this end. The individuality and independence of the school is realised through the individuality and independence of the head-teacher. The concept of the school as a community is bound up with that of the head-teacher as its leader. This romantic notion has its origins with what were called the 'autocrats of autocrats', the headmasters of the reformed Victorian public schools. The fusion of the idea of the school with the identity of its head-teacher has been expressed by King (1973) as a case of, 'L'école c'est moi'. Head-teachers are often judged by the success of their school; its failure is their failure.

Head-teachers expect both pupils and teachers to express loyalty to the school: 'Don't let the school down.' (These loyalties may endure and be expressed in the membership of former pupils' associations.) The idea of the pupil as a member of the community implies conformity and acceptance of the school's moral order and prevailing authority structure. The teacher's position as a member of the community is expressed in the diffuseness of his role, which in turn is related to the wide scope of interest he is expected to have in his pupils (see chapter 9). This is integral to the idea of pastoral care, which is sometimes called community care.

The expressive component of education is based on this ideology. The behaviour and disposition expected of pupils are justified in terms of their membership of the school community. Schools are transcendental organisations where attempts are made to create for present purposes situations which are believed to have future consequences. Pupil behaviour is regulated so that the school can be run smoothly and this experience is supposed to be a preparation for later life. Thus lateness rules are not only an attempt to bring learning groups together efficiently but also to internalise the importance of punctuality (King, 1973).

School rituals

Ritual consists of the use of symbols, which stand for, or represent, something else (King, 1973). Rituals may be ceremonials, where the symbol lies in their regularity and repetition, or emblems which are tangible, and include flags, badges and uniforms. The things symbolised tend to be diffuse and difficult to express precisely in words, often being strongly suffused with emotion, and considered to be very important by those who propagate the ritual – the teachers and head-teachers.

Speech days and prizes may symbolise the importance placed on academic success and approved behaviour. Many schools have mark reward schemes for both work and behaviour where merit is symbolised in the award of tokens – gold-edged cards in one school. The most important of the school rituals are those of the assembly and school uniform.

School assembly

School assemblies are clusters of ceremonial rituals. The following description gives the incidence of some of them in the assemblies of a sample of schools (King, 1973: the findings of this survey are reflected throughout this chapter).

The pupils enter the school hall supervised (93 per cent) by prefects (12 per cent) or teachers (82 per cent). They enter by age group (60 per cent) and take up special positions for their age group (88 per cent). Within age groups they enter by teaching group (43 per cent) and take up positions special to that group (53 per cent). The older pupils sit while the younger ones stand (15 per cent). The prefects take up their special positions (44 per cent). In the mixed schools, boys and girls enter separately (39 per cent) to take up separate positions (61 per cent), and the prefects enter separately by sex (52 per cent).

The teachers enter separately from the pupils (47 per cent), and take up their places on the platform (31 per cent). The head-teacher enters separately from all others (83 per cent). The pupils stand especially for his entrance (21 per cent), as do the teachers (28 per cent), and he takes up his position on the platform (92 per cent) behind a lectern (65 per cent). When the assembly is over the head-teacher leaves separately from all others (81 per cent), and the teachers process out (43 per cent). The pupils leave in the same groups they entered in.

This pattern of ceremonials is repeated in some schools five days a week for nine months of the year. Its structure symbolises the status system and authority relationships in the school. Pupils are differentiated by age, sex and imputed ability. Those with power over others – the prefects – exercise that power and present themselves as a separate group. The teachers, with more power and status, are separated and elevated from the pupils. The highest and the most conspicuously separated holds the most powerful position in the school: the head-teacher.

The head-teachers interviewed by King held that the school assembly had both religious and administrative or communication purposes but these were considered less important to what were felt to be its community fostering purposes, expressed in phrases such as 'brings everyone together', 'development of corporate attitudes', and most explicitly, 'develops a sense of community'. It is a daily reminder to the child that he or she is now, once again, a pupil. It 'gets pupils into the right frame of mind'. The communications of the school assembly are part of this. When the head-teacher makes an announcement to the whole school the fact that he is making it to everyone is part of the message. Sometimes this secular business is carried out by the deputy head, so emphasising the sacredness of the head-teacher's position.

There is a fusion between the religious, communal and authority presentation purposes of the school assembly. The school community is the body of worshippers, worship sanctifies the community, and the idea of the school as a community is legitimised by these connections. The authority of the head-teacher is fused with the authority of religion. Disrespectful behaviour in assembly is an offence to both the school and to the faith, to the head-teacher and to God. The school assembly is not only a daily reminder to the pupils of authority relationships, but also an assurance to the head-teacher that he retains his power. All authority has a tenuous quality and so the assembly is a test of the general allegiance of the pupils. In some schools pupils file quietly and obediently into the hall. In others they may be shouted at, cajoled or threatened into waiting in silence for the head-teacher's entry. These are remarkable feats of social control with the reluctant pupils outnumbering the teachers by twenty to one.

There is a certain irony in this. For head-teachers the school assembly symbolises consensus among the members of the school and their acceptance of his authority over them. When secondary pupils were asked their opinions about school most of them expressed approval of most of the things they were expected to do, but one exception was the assembly – used by head-teachers to promote consensus. This conflict of meanings illustrates the way that pupils and teachers may have different definitions of the same situation, and also how actions may have unintended and unrecognised consequences. Head-teachers intend the assembly to create consensus, but the outcome is discensus.

School uniform

The head-teachers' recognition of the school uniform as a symbol is made clear by this kind of comment: 'The wearing of the school uniform demonstrates respect for the things the school stands for'. What is symbolised may be inferred from the purposes it is supposed to serve. These include: removing social differences, promoting pride in the school, high morale and corporate spirit, and preventing competition in dress (especially between girls). Wood (1966) has suggested that uniform has basic role-defining function: 'it distinguishes home from school'. Defining the pupil as a member of the school community may subdue other identities that may form a threat to the pupil's allegiance to the school (for example, the teenager role), or the introduction of outside social and economic inequalities incompatible with the idea of a community.

Teachers and head-teachers seem to view the control they have over their pupils as being tenuous even mysterious. Willard Waller (1932) long ago pointed out that teachers exercise control by attention to detail. Teachers often interpret the negligent wearing of the uniform as an actual or potential rejection of the school. The uniform is visible and the manner it is worn susceptible to the most precise and reassuring inspection and regulation. 'Put your tie straight boy.'

Prefects

The prefectorial system is integral to the traditional idea of the school. Prefect–fagging systems existed in the public schools before Arnold's time, operating almost independently of the masters and head-masters, and prefects were often the leaders of rebellions (Mack, 1938). But these rebels were turned into the 'junior officers' of the system now institutionalised in many maintained schools.

Interviews with head-teachers show they attribute the same important expressive purposes to the system as did Arnold; to act as role models and as agents of social control. The former was expressed in phrases such as 'act as an example to younger pupils', and the latter in 'help maintain order'. These are well recognised by other pupils, and in one case study prefects were shown to be effective role models for younger pupils (King, 1969, ch. 5).

Authority relationships in schools are often ritualised. The office of prefect has its own emblems; ties, badges, sashes and girdles. Prefects are often marked off as a special status group in the ceremonials of assembly. Some schools hold prefect induction ceremonies, where the passing of the head-teacher's authority is symbolised by the shaking of hands and the presentation of emblems of office.

Some head-teachers have clear images of the ideal qualities of prefects; adult, polite, tolerant with common sense. They are chosen because they are thought to have these qualities, indicated by good behaviour, good performance in school, work and games. They are rewarded with privileges and possibly advantaged in their applications for jobs and continued education.

School bureaucracy

Weber regarded bureaucracy as the predominant form of organisation in modern society (for reference, see chapter 1). However, in non-sociological circles the term has pejorative connotations expressed in phrases such as 'red tape' and 'the bureaucratic machine', so that although technically all schools have bureaucratic features it is rare to hear the term used by teachers. But when they do 'administration', follow the timetable, or fill in reports, they are carrying out bureaucratic processes.

Weber used the term as an *ideal type* – a list of logically consistent features to be used in the study of actual organisations.

1. Tasks distributed as official duties carried out by technically qualified, specialist staff.
2. Formally established rules and regulations govern actions and decisions.
3. Hierarchical authority structure of offices.
4. Officials have an impersonal orientation to clients.

The last feature concerns the subjective meanings of bureaucrats. The first three concern the structure of relationships and these have been re-formulated by Pugh and his co-workers into:

1. Standardisation.
2. Formalisation – the use of paper (the number of filing cabinets is a crude index of bureaucratisation).
3. Specialisation.
4. Centralisation – the distribution of legitimate authority.
5. Configuration – the degree of 1, 2, 3 and 4, sometimes called the 'shape' of an organisation.
6. Flexibility – how the other features or dimensions change over time (Pugh *et al*, 1963; Hinings *et al*, 1967).

Bureaucratisation of teacher relationships and activities

Following Weber's ideal type, 'tasks distributed as official duties' is shown in the use of a school timetable which defines who teaches whom, what and where, at what time and for how long. All teachers in maintained schools are officially qualified (see chapter 9) and are sometimes specialised in particular subjects. In secondary schools instrumental specialisation is often matched by the expressive, in the creation of the pastoral care posts of tutor, head of house or year and counsellor. 'Formally established rules and regulations govern actions and decisions.' These include contracts, syllabuses, curricula, work sheets, schemes of work, weekly reports of work (in primary schools), staff handbooks, duty lists and mark sheets. These are all examples of formalisation: control by means of paper.

By law the head-teacher is at the top of the power pyramid; the centralisation of authority (King, 1968). Other ranks may descend from deputy heads, senior teachers, heads of department and House, teachers in-charge-of, down to plain teacher. The idea that teachers have an impersonal orientation towards their pupils may be queried, but such an orientation is expected as part of a sense of fairness when pupils are assessed in tests and exams.

Not all the activities of teachers are bureaucratically controlled – controls often generated by colleagues as well as superiors. In the classroom they retain a variable measure of autonomy concerning what they teach and how they teach it. These extra-bureaucratic activities are discussed in chapter 9.

It is often assumed that as organisations increase in size they become more bureaucratic. In a study of secondary schools Easthope (1975) found that increasing size was defined by head-teachers as a problem – a problem of communications. In response they often introduced elaborate committee structures or bulky staff handbooks. However, the more these bureaucratic devices were introduced the less satisfied were the teachers with their social relationships and the less their feelings of belonging to the school (community spirit). Committees were often introduced as ways of taking decisions more democratically, that is, the decentralisation of power. But when votes were taken on committees, dissent and conflict were made public and sometimes persisted. In some cases 'democratic' decisions were vetoed by the head-teacher.

The bureaucratisation of teacher–pupil relations and activities

The use of bureaucracy in the control of the learning and behaviour of pupils has been studied by King (1973), whose examples are quoted in this section.

Instrumental or learning activities may be standardised in the arrangements for homework, the marking of school work and the calculation of grades etc. at particular times. These activities are formalised, controlled by paper, by the use of homework timetables and diaries, and when test and exam results are put on to lists or reports.

Pupils' behaviour or expressive activities are extensively standardised. Over fifty rules were used dealing with behaviour on the school bus, walking to school, coming into school, use of cloakrooms, walking around the school, going to classrooms, breaktimes, dinnertime, and going home again. Some of these became formalised as written school rules, as did some punishments with the creation of detention books and late lists. The prevailing image of the ideal pupil that emerges is that he or she is punctual, well-behaved, neat and tidy, with a respect for ownership and property. Being well-behaved includes *not* smoking, fighting, chewing gum, dropping litter, being rude to teachers or the public. These might be considered more middle-than working-class characteristics, but most children from all classes find the rules regarding their behaviour reasonably acceptable. (They are part of the protestant ethic discussed in Hargreaves (1967, ch. 8); pupils' orientations are discussed in King, 1973.) However, teachers' assessments of their behaviour give lower ratings to the working class (e.g. National Child Development Survey, Plowden Report, 1967, vol. 2).

These rules are intended to control the pupils but they also control their teachers, who must see that the rules are obeyed, set and mark the homework, and fill in the reports. It is likely that some head-teachers introduce such things as homework diaries to control their teachers as much as the pupils.

The place of prefects in the formal authority structure of schools has already been mentioned. Studies of school or pupil councils by King (1973) and Chapman (1971) show that they provide pupils with very little power: things are discussed rather than decided; democracy is played at rather than enacted, the curriculum is seldom discussed – the teachers never.

Pupils are specialised by age, sex and imputed ability. These are dealt with in the following sections.

Age specialisation of pupils

Children were once regarded as miniature adults, now they are considered not only to become bigger as they grow but also to pass through stages of physiological, psychological and social development (Ariès, 1973). The educational *ideology of development* attempts to fit what children learn and how they are taught to their presumed stages of development (Bernstein and Davies, 1969). This is reflected in the age divisions within the educational system itself; nursery, infant, junior, secondary, higher and further education. Within schools it is shown in the age specialisation of the curriculum, some subjects are taught only to older pupils, and particularly in the age specialisation of learning groups. With the exception of vertical or family grouping in some primary schools, most groups are homogenous for age; schools are *age stratified*. This is not usual in America or in some European countries where standard or grade systems operate with promotion of the basis of work performance, as in the Victorian elementary schools.

The presumed greater maturity and responsibility of older pupils is reflected in the way there are fewer rules governing their behaviour and learning in school. On this basis they are made prefects; they also receive privileges, which are often the restoration of rights taken from younger pupils, such as not wearing the school uniform; age differences are also ritualised in the ceremonies of the school assembly (King, 1973).

Sex specialisation of pupils

Most primary schools are mixed, but a large proportion of secondary schools are single sex. Very young children are thought to have needs which are much the same for both sexes, but it is sometimes assumed that the differences between older boys and girls are such that they should receive different and sometimes separate educations.

Within mixed schools sex differentiation in the control of behaviour is shown in the sexes using different doors and cloakrooms, and queuing separately. The ceremonials of the school assembly may also be sex differentiating. Some mixed schools have separate sex classes for the same subjects especially PE and RE, and some subjects are taught exclusively to one sex (although this is changing by law – see chapter 10). Apart from reflecting presumed differences between the sexes some of these rules and distinctions in secondary schools are also concerned to control sexual liaisons between pupils. Holding hands is only permitted between girls. (King, 1973)

Mixed schools generally have less rules than single sex schools, and the extensive research of Dale suggests that pupils and teachers prefer mixed schools, when comparing their experiences with single sex schools (Dale, 1969).

Some further aspects of sex differences in education are returned to in Chapter 10.

Ability specialisation of pupils

A child's identity in terms of sex or age, is not created in school, although the experience of school may modify it, as when girls become the young ladies their teachers hope they will. All children acquire an *ability–identity* as a consequence of schooling. These are clearly created when children are sent to either grammar or modern schools, for the 'bright' and the 'average' respectively. Within the classroom the award of marks for good work and the public ranking of pupils in tests and exams also produce ability differentiation, as well as by teachers openly telling some that they are 'thick' and others they are 'clever'. Nash (1973, ch. 1) has shown that even when teachers attempt to disguise ability groups with the classroom the pupils are still well aware of their existence and how each individual ranks within the class. The clearest signal of pupil's ability identity is usually his learning group.

The variety of ways of grouping children for teaching and learning purposes is wide, including non-streaming (heterogeneous grouping or mixed ability grouping), banding (different status bands containing groups of equal status) setting (for particular subjects, either homogenous or heterogeneous for imputed ability), and options (incorporating some degree of pupil choice), as well as a combination of these. Most of the research has concentrated on streaming. This was discussed in Chapter 2 in terms of its possible contribution to social class differences in education, and a number of concommitants were described, including the over-representation of middle-class pupils in top streams, differences in pupil involvement across the streams and relationships with teachers. (Streaming and friendship choices are discussed in a later section.) Studies of junior schools by Lunn (1970) show that girls and older children are over-represented in top streams, but these have not been confirmed in secondary schools.

The meaning of streaming and other forms of ability grouping to teachers and head-teachers has been explored. At one level they justify it in terms of convenience, and also as meeting the 'needs' of individual pupils. (King found that every kind of secondary school grouping was justified by head-teachers in this way.) At another level it is based upon the same ideas that are used to justify and explain the connection between education and occupation discussed in Chapter 1. These are, that children differ in their abilities, and that high levels of ability are prerequisites for the adequate performance in high status occupations. Streaming and other forms of ability specialisation mediate in this relationship, as shown in this quotation from a head-teacher's notes for his staff: 'The fourth year will be split into three broad bands. The first band to be primarily academic . . . , the second band to be primarily technical (skilled and semiskilled artisans, not high grade technologists, who will come from the first band) and band three will be primarily general' (King, 1973, p. 116).

This explicit recognition of the selective and allocative functions of ability grouping shows that the stratified nature of the occupational structure is reflected in the ability stratification within the school. Thus streaming not only creates the ability identity of pupils but also signals their likely occupational destinies. In secondary schools King found the association between low stream and low involvement commoner among boys than girls. For boys, low stream status signals low status occupational destiny. This signal is less important for girls who have a stronger orientation towards marriage.

School friendships

The organisation of schools so far discussed has been concerned with *formal*, officially intended actions and relationships, although, as in the case of streaming and the school assembly, these may have unintended and unrecognised consequences. Children in school also enter into *informal* relationships with one another. (The informal relationships between teachers are discussed in chapter 9.) Many studies have shown that children choose friends from those with whom they interact most frequently, and from those they define as being similar to themselves. Thus most friends are also school-friends, who belong to the same teaching group and who tend to be at a similar standard in school work. Friends are usually of the same sex, girls' friendship groups being the smaller with rather more intense relationships. Friends do not usually belong to the same House, since House meetings are rare in most schools (King and Easthope, 1973). Friends formed in primary school tend to persist in the first few years of the secondary school (*ibid*, and Lacey, 1970, ch. 4).

Best friends in school often live near and are travelling companions. This may suggest that pupils choose friends from a similar social background to themselves. However, the evidence suggests that choices are made not so much on the basis of a friend's social class of origin but more on his or her social class of destiny, signalled by progress in school (Halsey and Gardner, 1953; Ford, 1970, ch. 5). Thus informal pupil relationships are a partial consequence of the formal processes and structures of the school, shown most clearly in studies of streaming.

Streams of different status not only differ in the relationships between teacher and pupils (see chapter 2), but also between the pupils themselves. This follows from the case-studies of Lacey (1970) and Hargreaves (1967). Hargreaves describes the 'academic' subculture of the top stream in which high informal status among the boys was given to those who worked hard and generally met the teachers' best expectations. In the bottom stream the 'delinquescent' peer group subculture gave high informal status to those boys who worked least hard and were most badly behaved in their teachers' estimates. Thus the relationships between pupils in top streams may make working hard doubly rewarding as it gains the approval of teachers and peers, but in the bottom stream hard work and good behaviour may be neither expected by the teachers nor approved by the peer group. There are, unfortunately, no comparable studies of peer groups in non-streamed classes.

Playgrounds are relatively free from formal control in that children are allowed to do things that would not be permitted in the classroom. Iona and Peter Opie's (1961) studies show the existence of a *playground culture* that is transmitted from older to younger children. This consists of songs, rhymes, games, lore (such as fainites), codes ('be a sport'), customs and stereotypes (nosey-parkers, cowardy-custards, tell-tales, fatty's and gingers). These may vary by the season (conkers, itching powder), and although subject to fashions and influenced by

Education

public events ('Hark the herald angels sing, Mrs Simpson's got our King', 1936) and incorporating heroes of the mass media ('We four lads of Liverpool are'), nevertheless has a consistency over time and from place to place.

These activities tend to confirm the formal and informal sex- and age-typing of the school and friendships groups, and form sources of knowledge about sex, death and disease sometimes denied them by adults, including teachers, possibly allowing them to express fears in an acceptable way. ('Look at the coffin, blooming great knobs on, Ain't it grand to be blooming well dead'.) They may also act as a safety valve in relation to adult authority figures ('Ladies and gentlemen take my advice, pull down your pants and slide on the ice').

Most of this interesting material was gathered in primary school playgrounds. Activities in those of mixed secondary schools probably include more boy-girl interaction (banter, name calling) leading to para-courtship.

School and youth culture

James Coleman (1961) studied the friendship groups in ten American high schools and concluded that they formed a youth subculture with norms and values at variance with those of adults, often being effectively anti-academic by their distribution of informal status and granting of group friendship on the basis of wearing the latest fashions and having a high dating-rating, rather than getting good grades for work.

The studies of streaming by Hargreaves (1967) and Lacey (1970) have shown the existence of antischool subcultures in the low streams of secondary schools but a great deal of research has contradicted Coleman's idea of a unitary anti-adult, anti-academic youth culture in this country. Studies of young people have shown how strongly conformist many are in terms of their general attitudes and social ambitions (Eppelard Eppel, 1966, Veress, 1962). Musgrove (1964) concluded that if any conflict exists between the generations, it comes mainly from the adult side. Sugarman (1967) investigated fourteen-year-old boys in four London Schools, and measured their commitment to the hypothesised youth culture in terms of responses to questions about smoking, going out with girls, pop music, and teenage fashions. Those with a high commitment to the 'teenage culture' tended to have what were judged to be poorer attitudes to school and conduct, and to have lower levels of academic achievement. These results may seem to confirm some of Coleman's ideas, but Sugarman also found that high commitment to the 'teenage culture' was particularly associated with working-class boys, and so he preferred to explain their poor conduct and achievement in social class terms. He concluded that, 'Youth culture is the culture of the non-mobile working class youth'.

Murdock and Phelps (1972) took Sugarman's analysis further, and in a study of a larger number of teenage school children make a distinction between 'street culture' and 'pop media culture'. The former is particularly associated with working class boys in urban areas, and uses the streets, cafés and other public places for its locale. It emphasises physical toughness, looking after yourself, and sticking with your mates. In contrast, the pop media culture is associated with girls, particularly from middle-class backgrounds. It is home-based and centres on records, magazines, television and radio programmes concerned with pop music. Murdock and Phelps suggest that adherence to either of these two cultures may be associated with rejection of school. In an associated piece of research Murdock and McCron (1973) describe a whole range of identities associated with pop music, ranging from the Top Twenty, followed mainly by younger girls, to progressive rock and underground music listened to by academic, often middle-class older boys. Statements about young people should be viewed witn the same caution as any that might be made about 'middle-aged people'; they are as socially diverse and varied as any other age group.

Maintained schools 6

The maintained schools are those which are financed wholly, or almost entirely, by public money. There are more than 30,000 in England and Wales, controlled by the local education authorities. There is not a state system of education in this country. Over 10,000 maintained (or 'grant-aided') schools are *voluntary schools*. Three different basic arrangements, *aided, controlled* and *special agreement*, allow voluntary agencies, principally the Church of England and the Roman Catholic Church, degrees of control over schools of their foundation, in return for financial support from the local authorities.

Maintained schools are officially classified using the criteria of age, ability and sex of their pupils. Children of all abilities between the ages of five and eleven go to primary schools, which are generally mixed schools. The fives to sevens are in separate infant schools or infant departments of primary schools, the over sevens may also be in separate junior schools. The secondary school system, for those over eleven, contains more single-sex schools, and until recently was fundamentally bipartite. Academically selective grammar schools received a minority of the secondary school population: the majority went to secondary modern schools. The small number of technical schools did not form a significant sector of a 'tripartite system', and were rather like second tier grammar schools. An increasing proportion of secondary schools are now comprehensive. (Statistics are published annually by the Department of Education and Science.)

working-class area, and a gratuitous Marxist perspective.

Primary schools are neighbourhood schools and so vary in their social compositions. Ashton and her fellow research workers (1975 ch. 2) found that head-teachers of schools in middle-class areas tended to stress intellectual development as an aim (not necessarily reflected in practice), whereas those in working-class areas stressed social development. There is a match between these results and Musgrove's, who found that parents in a middle-class area regarded it as their responsibility to teach their children how to behave, while those in a working-class area thought it was a job for the primary school (Musgrove and Taylor, 1969, ch. 3). Working-class children do receive the less favourable ratings for work and behaviour from their teachers.

Following the recommendations of the Plowden Report some junior schools have become Middle Schools with an eight to twelve age range. The eight-year-old entry was to fit in with the creation of First Schools; the retention until twelve was justified on the basis of 'more of a good thing'.

Grammar schools

Maintained grammar schools were created following the 1902 Education Act. They were not modelled on the shortlived higher elementary schools which specialised in science, engineering and mathematics, but, by general consensus, on the public schools, adult versions of their non-vocational curriculum and their [...] including prefects, House system and team games [...]5; King, 1969). This was also an acceptance of the [...]al education concerned with all round development [...]1974). Fees were required for entry for fear that the [...] be swamped by clever but 'uncultured' [...] children. The free places intended for them were [...]tained by middle-class children coached to [...]ere kept low and the introduction of selection [...]exams led to an increase in the proportion of [...]ils, many of whom later received grants tied to

Infant schools and departments

Infant education has special characteristics derived from origins quite different from those of the rest of the educational system. Its social history is marked by the names of ideologues such as Pestalozzi, Froebel, Montessori, the McMillan sisters and Suan Isaacs. Bernstein (1975) in a speculative essay suggests that a dissident middle-class group were important in this, but Nanette Whitbread's (1972) history makes clear that many of the innovators worked with working class slum children, and developed their educational ideas in connection with them.

The special ideologies of infant teachers are those labelled 'progressive', and endorsed by the Plowden Report, *Children and their Primary Schools* (1967). The official ideology of the Report is *child-centredness*. 'At the heart of the education process lies the child' (p. 7). The child, while possessing a unique individuality, is seen as passing through a naturally ordered sequence of physical, physiological and social development; the learning experiences are only successful when they are in harmony with the changing nature of the child. Young children are considered to be naturally curious, exploring and discovering things around them, learning best through play when they are happy and busy, and free to choose to do what is of interest to them. Education is seen as creating conditions which acknowledge these properties, and allow the full development of individual potential.

King, in a study (unpublished) of three large infants' schools, has shown how the acceptance of such ideas as real by teachers has consequences for their educational practices. The acquisition of the basic skills of reading and number are structured in an orderly sequence based on assumptions, often derived from Piaget, of the development of children's concepts. Infant teachers regard their young pupils as being basically innocent. It is not the case that they never do things that are defined as naughty, but that they cannot be blamed for this because they have not yet developed the capacity to control themselves. This is shown clearly in the oblique techniques of social control used by infant teachers. Little shaming and blaming are used. The verbal methods used instead include the no-need-to-answer-question, e.g. 'Are you getting on with your work?', said to someone obviously not doing so, and complete the sentence, e.g. 'And when we've finished our paintings we must . . .', pupils chorus, 'wash our hands'. Children quickly learn the nuances of meanings in the teacher's voice. These include the 'now we are going to do something exciting' voice, the 'slightly, aggrieved sad' voice, and the 'I am being very patient with you' voice (examples, perhaps, of restricted codes). Infant teachers also show professional equanimity, they are not upset when someone wets the floor; and professional affection, shown in their smiling faces and physical contact with children, holding hands and lap sitting, and in their use of endearments.

It is not too fanciful to see resemblances between infant teachers and the middle-class mothers of the Newsons' (1963, 1970, 1976) surveys referred to in Chapter 3: many infant teachers *are* middle-class mothers. Perhaps, not surprisingly, teachers gave more favourable ratings for work and behaviour to their middle-class pupils (King).

Following the recommendations of the Plowden Report (1967) some infant schools have become First Schools' retaining pupils until they are eight. This was based on a concern for slow readers who seemed to suffer in the transition from the infants to the juniors at seven.

Junior schools and departments

Child-centred progressive education is fairly securely institutionalised in infant schools and departments, but not so in junior schools and departments where its implementation is in conflict with traditional methods. This was centred on the streaming versus non-streaming controversy. The National Foundation for Educational Research's contribution to the Plowden Report showed streaming to be associated with older

teachers using more 'formal' methods and more physical punishments, with a low tolerance of noise, and sentiments in favour of the eleven-plus exam. Lunn (1970) was able to show that this sort of teacher could also be found in non-streamed classes; structural change does not always lead to teacher change. More schools have become non-streamed. The evidence to suggest this has advantages over streaming ·is not clear, though the two methods are justified in different ways (e.g. the 'social' advantages of non-streaming) and are therefore difficult to compare. This change is probably related to the increased numbers of comprehensive schools and the related abolition the eleven-plus.

The general 'progressive versus traditional methods' de has been fueled by the research of Bennett (1976). This that the progress of ten-year-olds taught by teachers def progressive on the basis of their answers to questions ab classroom practices, was slightly lower than for those traditional teachers. However, large measurements were found in a class taught by one 'progressive' te tion should be exercised in interpreting the general research. The children were not matched for s average measured ability was lower in pro suggesting they may be more working-class in c NFER in their survey for the Plowden Com streaming to be more common in schools se areas.) In addition the assessments of chi school classes were added together, so th gains are for groups of children never a As with the streaming/non-streaming argued that the aims of traditional and different and so the methods cannot

In quite a different kind of stu suggest that child-centred progre rejection of the authoritarian-eli formal approaches, a form of co on interviews with three teach a commitment to stay on at school and enter teacher-training, so that during the 1920s and 30s early leavers were more commonly middle-class fee-payers rather than working-class free places, an inversion of the usual class difference.

The 1944 Education Act led to the abolition of fees, and in the postwar period most early leavers were from working-class homes. This and their other characteristics were established by the *Early Leaving* report (CAC, 1954), which was concerned at the loss of educational talent (see chapter 2). In the 1960s several studies were concerned with the working-class experience of the grammar school. Jackson and Marsden's (1962) rather partial study concluded that, 'the grammar school has foundered on a rock – the working class'. In their descriptions of the tensions of working-class children moving between the different worlds of the school and their homes and neighbourhood, they were posing a cultural conflict theory.

In a study of a boys' grammar school King (1969) found that the values and interests that the teachers felt should be impor-tant to the boys were expectedly academic (e.g. an interest in books and scepticism), but also strongly middle-class in con-notation (e.g. watching BBC television was preferred to ITV, bridge was approved but solo disapproved). These values were more commonly held by second generation grammar school boys who were mainly middle-class. The early leavers, who were working-class first generation pupils from the bottom streams, did not hold these values to any great extent. However, their se-cond generation middle-class form mates, although no more in-volved in the school, did hold these values and did stay on into the sixth form.

The operation of the socially selective eleven-plus exam means that middle-class children are over-represented in the grammar schools, and the social class differences in the rates of staying on lead to their being even more over-represented in the sixth forms (Table 6.1). Before the introduction of comprehensive schools there was a large variation in the provision of grammar schools from one area to another – as low as 10 per cent of eleven-year-

Education

Table 6.1 *Social composition of schools*

| Pupil's father's occupation | Type of school | | | |
	Independent %	Grammar %	Modern %	All schools %
Professional and Managerial	79	26	5	13
Clerical and other non-manual	15	18	9	12
Skilled manual	6	44	55	51
Semiskilled manual	–	8	16	13
Unskilled manual	–	4	15	11

Source. Adapted from the Crowther Report (1960), 11.2, table 10.

olds with places, to as many as 40 per cent. Douglas (Robbins Report, 1963, App. 1) was able to show the areas with the more generous the provision, the more working class pupils were admitted and more stayed on into the sixth form. This is a clear example of more provision associated with more attainment.

Most pupils leave grammar school to take up non-manual middle-class occupations or continue their education to enter the higher ranks of the middle classes. King (1969) found that the boys in his case study school had a strong vocational evaluation of being at a grammar school which was highest for older boys. This was at variance with the values that their teachers felt should be important to them. Older boys actually read less books than younger ones, had less respect for honesty and truthfulness, and had less desire to help others, although they were more sceptical and viewed more teacher-approved programmes.

However, the academic regime of the grammar school, drawing on the legitimacy of the universities and professions the most successful leavers enter, does in itself signal its vocational importance. Lacey (1970, ch. 4) found that first-year boys new to academic competition often took some time to settle down, also partly because of their transformation from top pupils in their primary schools to sometimes being a mere B or C streamer. More recently King (1973) has shown that grammar schools have moved towards non-streaming for the first few years, because head-teachers felt it to be invidious to further select from their already selected intake.

Compared with other secondary schools King (1973) found grammar schools to have the most extensive prefectorial systems, a reflection of the high status of the sixth form. The authority positions of head-teacher, teacher and prefect were much ritualised. Pupils were often controlled by formalisation – the bureaucratic use of paper, as on notice boards, lists of rules and homework diaries. This kind of control is based on the assumption that the pupils can read, will read, and will act on what they have read. It is an impersonal form of bureaucratic authority which permits messages to flow only from the superordinate sender to the subordinate receiver.

Secondary modern schools

Secondary modern schools have their origins in the elementary schools set up by the 1870 Education Act, which, by concentrating on the three Rs, were intended to produce a more useful labour force without actually educating them. After the 1902 Act, creating the grammar schools, and the Hadow Report of 1926, senior elementary schools catering for eleven- to fourteen-year-olds emerged, and these were the immediate precursors of the modern schools set up after the 1944 Act (Maclure, 1969). The earlier Norwood Report (1943) had spuriously posed the existence of three types of child, the academic, the technically able and those good with their hands. Although not directly endorsed by the Act, LEAs acted up on these ideas, and the modern schools were intended to provide a general non-academic, non-vocational education. With great piety it was officially intended that there should be 'parity of esteem' between the different kinds of secondary school (Banks, 1955).

Most modern school pupils are from working-class homes (Table 6.1) and leave school to enter mainly working-class occupations, many of which require no educational qualifications. Nevertheless in the 1950s some modern schools, sometimes clandestinely to avoid LEA disapproval, began to enter small numbers of pupils for public examinations such as O level and the Royal Society of Arts, often with remarkable success. The studies of Turner (1969) and Taylor (1963) show that the pressures for this change came from teachers, discontented with the diffuseness of the official purpose of a general education and anxious to set goals for their more able pupils which would enhance their career chances, from aspiring and interested parents, and from the pupils themselves. These examinees stayed on voluntarily for a fifth year before the school-leaving age was raised to sixteen in 1972. The evidence suggests they were mainly from lower middle- and upper working-class families.

The Crowther Report (1959) and the Beloe Report (1960) recommended the setting up of an examination system for children below O level ability. After the establishment of the Schools Council for the Curriculum and Examinations in 1964, the Certificate of Secondary Education was introduced in 1965. The CSE is administered by fourteen regional boards with strong teacher representation, and its highest grade is supposed to be the equivalent of an O level pass. The coming of CSE created a new category of pupils in the schools: the non-examinees. These are the pupils who before 1972 left after four years of secondary schooling, and were characteristically from semiskilled or unskilled manual workers' homes. As the novels of the period (e.g. Blishen, 1969) record, they sometimes constituted a chronic, even acute, problem of social control within some schools. It was the education of these pupils that the Newsom Committee reported on in 1963. In striking contrast to the seven-volume Robbins Report on higher education which appeared in the same year, the Newsom Report is a single volume. It reviewed and endorsed a wide range of methods used with the less able pupils, and pinned much hope on the establishment of better material facilities, particularly in the slum areas, where what came to be called 'Newsom children' predominate. The surveys of the report were poorly done, and their thin results, supplemented by some from the excellent surveys of the Crowther Report, are reported using the crude stereotypes of Brown, Jones and Robinson children. However, as a teachers' handbook the report has been a source of legitimacy for all kinds of 'Newsom' schemes.

These innovations were a response to what was defined as a problem of social control of the 'less able' pupils, with whom the traditional curriculum and teaching methods seemed only to work when associated with the increasingly unacceptable use of strict discipline. The response was to present them with a curriculum based on assumptions of what they would find interesting and useful, including choosing to acquire quasi-vocational skills such as car driving and maintenance, and the preparation for adult life through studies of baby care and income tax (King, 1973). This child-centred education draws on the legitimacy of the pupils themselves, who having chosen to do what interests them are supposed to present less problems of control.

Some of this concern is reflected in the organisation of modern schools. King (1973) found that the pupils were controlled by more rules covering both work and behaviour than those in other secondary schools. This indicates the way that good behaviour and work are considered to be rather scarce commodities in some of these schools. This is also shown in the extensive ritualisation of academic success and good behaviour in such schools, which had more symbolic mark reward systems and prizes than others. The ideology of the school as a community implies consensus, and so it is precarious where there is conspicuous conflict in a school. In boys' secondary modern schools, where the prescription of the allegiance-forming uniform is lowest, and where the teachers' definition of conflict is shown in the widespread use of caning, head-teachers were less likely to refer to the school as a community, but to substitute a custodial ideology drawing upon

81

ideas emphasising containment and firm discipline with strong military connotations. In one such school pupils were actually marched from class to class.

An ideology found only in modern schools is an ameliorative one, which is an attempt to revive the pupils' self-esteem despite the low status of their school, by presenting the provision of external exams as a second chance of success.

> I think it important that you should be fully aware that although not selected for a grammar school, your child has a full range of opportunities, academic, social and vocational, for which the school makes full preparations. (Head-teacher's letter to parents of new pupils, King, 1973.)

Comprehensive schools

The idea of a national system of non-selective secondary schools has its origins with left wing political groups and activists in the period between the world wars (Rubenstein and Simon, 1969). Although the Spens Report on secondary education in 1938 briefly commented on what was then called the 'multi-lateral school', following the 1944 Act and abolition of grammar school fees, the LEAs, including the Labour controlled ones, set up bipartite systems of grammar and modern schools. However, ten comprehensive schools had been created by 1950 and the number has increased so that the prospect of a national system is now in sight.

In 1965 the Labour Secretary of State issued Circular 10/65 which requested LEAs to submit plans for the reorganisation of secondary education in their areas along comprehensive lines. Up to that time it was not necessarily only Labour controlled LEAs that had created such schools, but after this the 'rebels' who did not submit plans were more commonly Conservative. In 1970 the Conservative Secretary of State rescinded circular 10/65 with circular 19/70, but with another change of government circular 4/74 requested LEAs to submit their reorganisation plans by the end of 1974. The few remaining rebels will be compelled to reorganise with the passing of 1976 Education Act.

The introduction of comprehensive schools has been a struggle between power groups at the local and national levels. The idea of comprehensive education has also been advanced and criticised by many interest groups. The groups in favour include the Campaign for Comprehensive Education and the Confederation for the Advancement of State Education; those against include the National Education Association and the Black Paperites. The early arguments for comprehensive education concentrated as much on what were thought to be the defects of the selective system of grammar and modern schools, as upon the supposed merits of comprehensive schools. Drawing on the surveys of the *Early Leaving*, Crowther and, later, Robbins reports, a large wastage of educational talent had been shown to occur, particularly among working-class children. This wastage has been attributed to the operation of the secondary selection procedure, shown by Douglas, Floud and Halsey (1968) and others to contain a social selection element favouring middle-class children, particularly at the borderline level, and to the value system of the grammar school, which Jackson and Marsden (1962) and King (1969) have shown to be unacceptable to some working-class pupils. A major ideological justification of the comprehensive system is that it will widen educational opportunities and reduce the class gap in educational attainment.

Julienne Ford (1970) attempted to put some of the claims for a comprehensive system to the test. She examined the pro-comprehensive school literature to produce five propositions: that it will produce a greater development of talent, provide a greater degree of social equality of opportunity, raise working-class levels of occupational aspirations, promote social mixing and the conception of society as a flexible hierarchy rather than a rigid dichotomy ('them and us'). She operationalised these propositions in the form of items in a questionnaire which was administered to pupils in one modern, one grammar and one comprehensive school. She interpreted the results to indicate that none of the five propositions was confirmed.

Reservations must be expressed about this claim. It could be argued that these five effects would only be apparent in a national system of exclusively comprehensive schools. If this is so, then the propositions could only be tested using a 'before and after comprehensivisation' research design, which would have many methodological problems. If it is accepted that the propositions may be validly tested in the present mixed system of secondary schools, then it would be necessary to choose the sample schools with great care. As might be expected the social class and ability compositions of the grammar school actually chosen were higher than those of the modern school. However, the social composition of the comprehensive was more working-class than that of the modern school, and its ability composition only a little more favourable, and so it was not fully comprehensive in these respects.

Other research by Douglas *et al* (1968), King (1973) and Holly (1965) does confirm that existing comprehensive schools do not necessarily raise the occupational and educational ambitions or school involvement of their working-class pupils to middle-class levels. Unlike Ford (1970), Miller (1958) found evidence of more social mixing in comprehensives than in other secondary schools, although using a different method of measurement. Pedley (1970) presented some evidence that comprehensive schools can provide more educational opportunities, but Davis (1967) has argued that the development of exams in modern schools might have allowed the bipartite system to do as well. Neave (1975) has shown that even eleven-plus failures can get to university through the comprehensive system. A problem in comparing the academic outputs of schools is that many existing comprehensives are in areas with grammar schools, and as Monks (1968) has shown, have more working-class pupils and less 'bright' pupils than may be expected.

The argument against the comprehensive school often concentrates on size, which would have to be big if it were to support a viable sixth form and present pupils with a wide choice of subjects and courses. It was also feared that there would not be enough specialist teachers available to staff a national system of 'all-through' eleven-to-eighteen schools (King, 1976, chs 5, 12). However, although the early schemes of reorganisation used all through schools, they are now less common. This is based on two assumptions; that such schools must be large and that they require expensive new buildings. Split-site arrangements using existing buildings are not favoured, partly because this denies the concept of the school as a unified community.

Following the lead given by Circular 10/65 many forms of comprehensive schools now exist. These include two-tier systems of junior and senior schools, three-tier systems involving middle schools, and sixth form centres in all-through schools receiving pupils from fifth forms from the same school and from other schools without sixth forms. Perhaps the most controversial have been the sixth form colleges. These seem to have economic advantages in terms of the way they may use existing buildings and in the concentration of scarce specialist teachers to teach only older pupils.

The corollary of any form of separate sixth form provision is the short course comprehensive for eleven- or twelve-to-sixteen year-olds. The research reported by King shows that most of the fears about the academic viability of such schools, in terms of provision of courses and examination success, are not substantiated in at least one local education authority (King, 1974; 1976, ch. 6). In the absence of sixth-formers such schools are still able to carry out most of the activities considered desirable in English education. Today's fifth-formers can lead as well as yesterday's sixth. In addition, there are also a few tertiary or comprehensive colleges, usually based on former colleges of further education, which provide for all the post-sixteen education in the area, both academic and vocational, full- and part-time; this is arguably the most comprehensive form of organisation (King, 1976, chs 9, 12).

In urban areas LEAs have different policies for allocating children to comprehensive schools. 'Banding' involves allocation so that each school receives a similar proportion of children from a number of ability bands defined by test results. Because of the relationships between measured ability and social class, the schools will tend to have similar social compositions, and, because of the relation between social class and early leaving, their sixth forms will be of a similar size. Since older pupils accrue more points used in the allocation of resources of money and staff, these will also be evenly distributed. This method of allocation clearly relates to what Marsden (1969) has called the meritocratic version of the comprehensive ideology; providing equal opportunities for pupils to succeed irrespective of background. An alternative to banding is zoning or recruitment on a neighbourhood basis. Its protagonists accept that neighbourhood schools would sometimes be 'one class' schools and argue that they should be given extra resources to compensate for the economic disadvantages of the small sixth forms they are likely to have. King (1974) has pointed out that short-course neighbourhood schools would not vary in the allocation of resources since they have no sixth forms.

The idea of the neighbourhood school is often linked to what Marsden (1969) calls the egalitarian version of the comprehensive ideology, which looks to the comprehensive system as an agency of social change in bringing about a classless society. The supposed process by which this would come about is through children's experience of being educated with others from different social backgrounds. King and Easthope (1973) have shown that the more mixed the social composition of a school, the more friendships are made between the social classes. Neighbourhood schools, being rather socially homogeneous, would be associated with less social mixing and therefore, according to the theory, be less effectively egalitarian than banded schools.

Many elements of the internal organisation of comprehensive schools express these ideologies. King (1975) found that they used double entry exam policies more often than other schools, entering pupils for CSE and GCE in the same subjects (shown to be advantageous by Joan Fry, 1974), or even the same subject for two different GCE boards, in order to maximise exam achievement. There was limited use of rituals to celebrate academic success. Speech day exam prizes and work-mark competitions were thought to discourage the less able; instead prizes were more often awarded for school service.

The size of all-through schools is viewed ambivalently by their head-teachers (King, 1973). On the one hand it is celebrated in allowing the provision of a wide range of subjects and courses. On the other it is seen as a threat to the idea of the school as a community – the fear that pupils will feel lost in a large organisation and possibly present problems of control. In response to this there has been a strengthening of the pastoral care system, by the creation of tutorial groups, sometimes on a House basis. In this the House system has been reformed from something revived once a year for sports day, into units for administration, pastoral care and even teaching, so that heads of Houses have become surrogate head-teachers. The studies of King (1973) and Ross *et al* (1972) suggest that these measures are reasonably successful, King has shown that larger schools are not necessarily associated with more bureaucratic control of the pupils, but Easthope (1975, ch. 6) found this to be so with respect to teachers (see chapter 5). In larger and more bureaucratic schools teachers reported less feelings of belonging and less satisfaction with their relationships with colleagues. Perhaps there is a problem of pastoral care for teachers in large comprehensive schools?

Over 94 per cent of children go to maintained schools. A few are educated at home, or, for a number of reasons, are incapacitated and unable to go to any kind of school, but most of those who do not attend maintained schools are pupils of private schools. These are schools which are outside the control of the local education authorities and where most pupils are fee paying. There are about 3,000 schools in this category, and they vary from small day proprietary schools for mixed juniors to the large and sometimes ancient boarding schools, known as public schools.

Public schools

It is not possible to define exactly what is meant by a public school. For the sake of this discussion they will be defined as private boarding schools for boys or girls of secondary school age, which are members of one or more of the various protective associations of the higher status sector of private education (the Head Masters' Conference, the Governing Bodies Association, the Association of Governing Bodies of Girls' Public Schools), in all, about 300 schools.

Public schools are boarding schools for the children of the well-to-do, and most of their distinctive features rise from these two factors. Virtually all their pupils are from middle-class homes, mainly with professional or managerial fathers and their families are for the most part in good cultural continuity with the school, often having received the same sort of education themselves (Kalton, 1966). The activities of the school are legitimised by the approval of the parents. This is implied in their having chosen to send their children to such schools. These schools have a high social status, often at a national level of recognition in view of their wide geographical intake. This status is related to the social origins of the pupils. Because of the relationship between social class and measured intelligence (chapter 2), most of these pupils are of what has been called 'grammar school standard'. As the Kalton (1966) survey shows, very few of them have intelligence quotients below 100. This, together with their educationally favourable backgrounds, means that the rate of academic success for such pupils tends to be high, and this too contributes to the status of the schools.

Public schools are selective, and this selectivity is based principally on the ability of the parents to pay the fees. As this selection often takes place some years before the pupils enter the school, it is in effect the parents who are selected; thus preference is often given to the child of a former pupil, or to pupils from particular preparatory schools with which special relationships exist. All public school candidates sit the Common Entrance Examination, and about 80 per cent of them pass at the first attempt. Since the public schools mark the papers of their aspiring preparatory school candidates each school is able to set its own academic standards. Thus among public schools there is a status hierarchy based on two, sometimes related, criteria: the performance required in the Common Entrance Examination, and the size of the school fees.

Their anomalous name, public schools which are exclusively private, has its origins with the schools set up for 'poor scholars' in the fourteenth and fifteenth centuries under Church and royal patronage. By the mid-eighteenth century these had been almost completely taken over by the sons of the aristocracy and gentry, who had previously been educated by servants or tutors. The 'poor scholars' were catered for in a 'separate second grade department' and eventually in newly created day schools to protect the charity foundation; for example Harrow established the Henry VIII Grammar School. As the Headmaster of Repton put it, 'I never saw a man yet who would send his boy to school to associate with those lower than himself' (Simon, 1966; the source of contemporary quotations in this chapter). The 'insubordination, idleness, insolence, lying, gluttony, ignorance and vice' of these social betters led to the reforms of Arnold and others, outlined in chapter 5. The demand for a gentleman's education for the sons of the newly emerging middle classes led to an increase in the number of schools in the second half of the nineteenth century.

A number of studies have been made of contemporary boys' public schools. The survey by Weinberg (1967) and the case study by Wakeford (1969) draw on Erving Goffman's (1969) idea of the total institution, who originally applied it to asylums, but suggested it also may be applied to monasteries, reformatories, prisons and boarding schools: 'A total institution may be defined as a place of residence and work where a large number of like situated individuals, cut off from the wider society for an appreciable period of time, together lead an enclosed formally administered round of life.'

Much of the organisation of the schools relates to their total nature. Each day is formally arranged by a timetable so that it is known what each pupil is doing at any time, even when he must pursue a recognised hobby. Pupils are subject to a formal round of life under fairly constant supervision. The smooth running of the school puts a premium on conformity, which may be obtained by stripping away the pupil's personal identity by the use of uniforms and the propagation of emotional neutrality in personal relationships, as part of what Lambert (1975) calls the 'stiff-upper-lip syndrome'. Their isolation from family and neighbourhood allows the pupils only a limited range of social relationships. Even within the school the organisational rule may be to effectively deny brother/brother relationships because this would cut across the fairly rigid age stratification pattern with its elite sixth form and attendant fags. With so few formally permitted affective outlets it is not surprising that boys in these single-sex public schools have an increased susceptibility to homosexuality, acknowledged by half the senior boys in Lambert's survey. Matron and the housemaster's wife are clearly not very effective girlfriend substitutes (Young Woodley not withstanding).

The supervision duties of the staff, themselves mainly ex-public school boys, are extensive; this, in part, accounts for the low teacher/pupil ratio in such schools. Little evidence exists to show that this ratio, or the boarding system it is associated with, leads to greater academic success on the part of the pupils. (The Kalton survey indicated that the few day public schools do as well in terms of examination passes as the boarding public schools, if not better.) Prefectorial and House systems form important parts of the formal organisation. The creation of prefects not only enables the promotion of official role models and agents of social control, but also sponsors potential social deviants into elite positions of status and privilege. The House is often the living and sometimes teaching unit within the school, often with a subsystem of House prefects and other positions. A housemaster may occupy a position of considerable power within the school, often with a great deal of autonomy in regulating House affairs, even to the extent of selecting pupils without reference to the headmaster. Games, played nearly every afternoon, promote House and School pride, and are one side of the model of 'muscular Christianity' completed by compulsory chapel.

The public schools probably exhibit the phenomenon of the collapsing of ends and means more than any other kind of British school. The means of social control and cultural transmission become ends in themselves. The emphasis on conformity, loyalty, acceptance of authority and the concealment of emotions are valued as important to the smooth running of the school, and as desirable in themselves.

Perhaps the most glamorous aspect of the public school, well known through Billy Bunter and Tom Brown, are the informal activities of pupils, what Goffman (1969) calls the 'underlife'. Dormitory feasts and night escapades do occur, sometimes known to but ignored by staff whose own school careers often included such activities. The pupil peer group is powerful in extracting its own conformities in dress, speech and manner, and in weilding its own effective sanctions. New boys, variously called brats, ticks, squits, scum and scugs, have to learn these ways (Weinberg, 1967; Wakeford, 1969). Not surprisingly, a large proportion of the boys surveyed by Lambert (1975) reported they were homesick for a year or more.

Public schools for girls are less numerous and more recent in origin. (Even the rich have their priorities.) The study by Wober (1971) showed these to be organised around the idea of the education of young ladies, to be compared with the 'gentlemanly ideal' of the boys' schools. Most girls conformed to the tight formal controls (different pairs of shoes to be worn on different occasions, even two kinds of gloves), but Wober found little evidence of homosexuality, or the kind of underlife flourishing in boys' schools. (Perhaps this was because Wober is a man?)

Most leavers from the boys' public schools eventually enter occupations similar to those of their fathers, many having gone to university first, their status confirmed by the receipt of education symbolic of their class. There is no doubt that special relationships exist between some public schools and certain colleges of Oxford and Cambridge which grant a definite preferment towards public school applicants, who make up more than one-third of the students. Ex-public school boys also occupy many positions of power and prestige in business and public life (see Table 7.1).

Various explanations may be posed to account for the distribution of power and prestige to such a small minority group. The least likely is that these positions have been gained by educational merit alone. It is commonly assumed that a public school education is advantageous independently of academic success, a qualification in itself indicating the possession of desirable character traits. However, the attribution of these traits is made largely by those who suppose that they have them too: ex-public school boys selecting who should join the elite,

Table 7.1 *Public school pupils in various social positions (percentages)*

Fourteen-year-olds in school	2.6	Senior service officers	55.0
Seventeen-year-olds in schools	9.3	Directors of firms	70.8
University students	15.6	Bishops (C of E)	75.0
Oxford and Cambridge students	35.1	Judges and QCs	79.2
Labour MPs (1966)	19.5	Senior doctors	68.0
Conservative MPs (1966)	76.6	Directors of Bank of England	76.5
Labour Cabinet (1967)	42.0	University professors	32.5
Conservative Cabinet (1963)	90.9	Oxford and Cambridge professors	49.3

Source. Derived from Public Schools Commission, *First Report* (1968) Vol. II, App. 8, sec. 4.

and, therefore, self-perpetuating groups. This is the 'old boy' network. The assumption that it is difficult for those without a public school education to enter certain positions may deter them from trying. It could also be argued that the powerful are so because of their family backgrounds and social connections, and that their having been to public schools makes little contribution to the state of affairs but simply draws attention to it. This would scarcely explain why 35 per cent of Conservative MPs in 1966 came from just six of the 'top' schools, and why in 1963 they provided 64 per cent of the Conservative cabinet (Public Schools Commission, First Report, vol. 1, App. 8, sec. 4).

Concerns about this domination of elite positions have existed for a long time in the Labour party and this led to the setting up of the Public Schools Commission which reported in 1968–70. Although enquiries were made into the connections between the public schools and general social order, the Commission concentrated on their educational divisiveness. The four important ways were: social (they are almost exclusively middle class in composition); ability (few of their pupils are below average intelligence); sex (they are nearly all single-sex schools); and boarding (which divides pupils from their families and the local community). The Commission suggested that a reduction of social divisiveness and compatibility with a comprehensive system would be produced by suitable and willing public schools being 'integrated' through admission of assisted pupils from maintained schools to at least half of their places. The integrated schools would provide CSE courses for some of the less able assisted pupils who would be so assisted only on the basis of their 'need' for boarding education. The present autonomy of the LEAs and individual public schools in the sponsoring and acceptance of pupils would be reduced by giving oversight to the integration programme to a Boarding Schools Corporation, responsible to the Secretary of State. There are no good reasons for supposing this policy, similar to the more modest one of the Fleming Report (1944), will be implemented. None of the parties concerned welcomed the report, the cost of the integration programme would be high, and there is perhaps now a feeling that since abolition of the public schools seems politically untenable, isolation is a better alternative to integration.

Isolation is the key to policies that have actually been enacted. Ironically, some of the money going to the public schools is public money, and recent Labour governments have produced legislation to reduce such things as the tax advantages of composition fees, educational endowments and covenants, where, for example, companies pay for the education of the children of their top employees and receive tax relief. The schools with charity status receive rate relief – the playing fields of Eton are subsidised by the rate-payers of Slough.

The effect of the public schools on the maintained system of education is also important. Those of the nineteenth century were used as models for maintained secondary schools. Brian Jackson (1963, Appendix) lays the blame for this on the influence of Robert Morant, the chief civil servant of the new Board of Education. An ex-public school boy, his purpose was to make sure that 'the education system of the twentieth century should be modelled on schools like his own'. The studies of Mitchell (1964) and Banks (1955) suggest this is an overstatement, but it

94

does lead to a pertinent question. How many chief education officers, members of education committees, heads of maintained schools, Her Majesty's Inspectors, and under secretaries of the DES went to public schools? Perhaps more pertinently; how many send their own children to such schools, and how many to the maintained schools they run and are responsible for?

Preparatory schools

The 400 registered preparatory schools act as agencies for the socialisation of children in preparation for places in public schools. Most of their pupils, aged between eight and thirteen, come from private kindergartens and nurseries, which sometimes form a junior non-boarding section to the preparatory school. Many preparatory schools have special relationships with particular public schools (some may be junior sections of public schools), and in general their organisational regimes tend to resemble those of the public schools, especially in the case of boarding preparatory schools.

The preparatory school system may be seen as part of a chain of agencies for socialising the children of the rich. The families of the wealthy tend to be less child-centred than most middle-class families: the young children are effectively reared by paid servants, nannies, even *au pair* girls, and may only have limited contact with their parents. The emphasis on self-reliance and obedience generated in the family is continued in the kindergarten and the preparatory school, so that the social isolation of the public school comes as less of a shock to most of these children, who are encouraged from a very early age to behave as miniature adults. However, their mothers did often report distress when they sent their children away to school (Lambert *et al*, 1975).

Progressive schools

A small number of private co-educational boarding schools are referred to as progressive schools. The best known are Summerhill and Dartington. In these schools the traditional forms of social control associated with the public schools are not used. There is no official school uniform, although the pupils tend to generate their own norms of dressing, which may be enforced by just as effective and powerful informal sanctions as the official uniform of a traditional school. Pupils may be given a great deal of personal autonomy and a measure of privacy in separate rooms. This kind of provision is permitted by the very heavy fees. These schools are usually organised around some special ideology of the charismatic founder, often stressing individuality, freedom and creativity.

The continued existence of such schools is assured by parental demand. Wealthy parents with doubts about public school education may prefer one of these schools for their child. As this choice indicates, these parents are likely to be rather unusual middle-class people, often with academic or artistic occupations. They form a powerful source of legitimation for whatever unusual activities the school promotes, be it the rejection of examinations or mixed nude bathing. The kind of organisation associated with these schools is related to their unusual pupil intake, and the autonomy granted to older pupils is usually preceded by many years of socialisation in the junior school. The idea of the school as a community is elevated to a utopia where school represents the ideal society rather than a preparation for the society outside.

Other private schools

More than 2,000 other private schools exist in Britain, and they present an enormous variety. Some are boarding only, others are mixed day and boarding, others are exclusively day schools. Some are mixed juniors and girls, others single-sex. Between them they cater for the age range between five and eighteen. Some are well equipped, others operate in private houses. Many are proprietary schools, and most are small.

The pupils of these schools are likely to come from middle-class homes, where the parents can only afford modest fees compared with those for public schools. The frequent hope of these parents is that such schools will confer educational advantages on their children and also that the school will protect them from the influence of children from working-class homes whom they might have met in the local maintained schools. Children who have not gained a grammar school place are sometimes spared the shame of the secondary modern school by being sent to fee-paying 'independent grammar schools'.

These schools, especially the small proprietary ones, often have to struggle for economic viability; more than a thousand have closed in the last fifteen years. Unlike some of the public schools they cannot be registered as charities, and so gain rates exemption, nor do they have rich trusts or covenants. They must usually budget on their fees alone. As the wage bill is the biggest item of expenditure in any school system, they often have poorly qualified staff. This general shortage of money also shows itself in the way in which these schools economise on domestic staff by making the pupils pursue character-building activities such as bed-making, gardening and washing the headmaster's car.

There has recently been a tightening of what little central control exists over such schools. In 1967, following the conviction for cruelty of a joint principal of an independent school, the Secretary of State instituted a confidential enquiry. A consequence of its report was the announcement that all independent boarding schools would have to reach the standard requirements to be considered 'efficient'. It seems likely that those which cannot meet the standard expected close down rather than be brought to the test. This is probably another factor in the falling numbers of such schools.

Direct grant schools

This is an obsolescent category. About 2 per cent of children of secondary age go to about 200 direct grant schools. They occupy an anomalous position in the educational system in that although they are financed from both private and public sources they are almost entirely privately controlled. They are mainly single-sex, day and/or boarding schools, mostly recruiting pupils at eleven. Some of these pupils are fee payers, others are sponsored by the LEA. In return for accepting those pupils whose fees are paid by the LEA, the school receives a grant directly from the DES. Yet other pupils receive some assistance with fees from public funds, both central and local. Altogether about 60 per cent of the pupils in direct grant schools receive some kind of financial assistance from public sources, but the local authority is not represented on the boards of governors of such schools and has virtually no control over the school activities.

Most of the boarding direct grant schools are similar in their organisation to public schools, and some of them are in fact members of the Head Masters' Conference, which is often used in a definition of a public school. The day direct grant schools, like the few day public schools (using the HMC definition), are run rather like maintained grammar schools, but are likely to have a much larger proportion of middle-class pupils than most maintained grammar schools, mainly due to the fee-paying element which is almost exclusively middle-class. The mean measured ability of pupils in direct grant schools is likely to be higher than that in many maintained grammar schools, in that the pupils sponsored by the local authority have often been the most 'able' of the current year's eleven-plus cohort (a process known in maintained schools as 'cream-whipping'). The favourable social and ability compositions of direct grant schools accounts for the high levels of academic success in such schools. Evidence submitted to the Public Schools Commission suggest that pupils in these schools do as well as may be expected at O level when compared with those in maintained grammar schools, but less well, by comparison, at A level.

The Second Report of the Public Schools Commission (1970) recommended that they be given the option of becoming either parts of comprehensive systems, which only a few have done voluntarily, or becoming entirely privately financed. This was implemented in 1975 when the Secretary of State announced that it was to be the last year of the award of the direct grant, although existing free place holders will be supported until the end of their school careers.

Further and higher education refer to post-school formal education. Higher education is usually full-time education leading to a degree or its equivalent. Colleges of education, polytechnics and universities are its major agencies. Further education refers to both full- and part-time education, which may or may not lead to qualifications below degree level. The main agencies of further education are the technical colleges as well as specialised colleges for agriculture and other occupations.

Universities

There are forty-one British universities. Oxford and Cambridge date from the fourteenth century, and until the foundation of the universities of London and Durham in the early nineteenth century they dominated British academic life, catering for the education of the aristocracy, gentry and clergy, and organised around the ideology of the *cultivated man*. The larger civic universities, such as Manchester, Liverpool, Leeds, Birmingham and Bristol, began as local enterprises and through their industrial links introduced scientific and engineering studies, which together with the professional studies of law and medicine introduced by London and Durham, were part of a new ideology, that of the education of the *specialist man*. The smaller civic universities, including Exeter, Southampton and Nottingham, were originally university colleges of London but were given independent charters in the 1950s (Halsey and Trow, 1971).

In the early 1960s about 4 per cent of young people were at universities, but this had doubled by the end of the decade. Three factors contributed to this, the bulge, the trend and ideology.

When birth rates are plotted as a graph an increase over several years appears as a *bulge*. There have been two bulges in the birth rate in the postwar period; the first was immediately after the war, the children entering the primary schools in the early 1950s, the secondary schools in the later 1950s, and higher education in the mid-1960s. The birth rate fell in the 1950s until an upward trend led to the second bulge which reached its peak in 1964. The children of this second bulge were passing through the primary schools in the 1960s and are now in the secondary schools, where the peak will pass in the early 1980s. Birth rates have been low in recent years and there is no sign of an increase yet.

The *trend* refers to the increased tendency for young people to choose to stay longer in full-time education. The proportion gaining two or more A levels has tripled in twenty years. The ideology, of *meritocracy*, was endorsed by the Robbins Report (1963): '. . . courses of higher education should be made available for all those who are qualified by ability and attainment to pursue them and who wish to do so'. The policy was put into practice and, fed by the children of the first bulge and the trend, an expansion of higher education took place, including the foundation of new universities, like Sussex and York, and the conversion of six colleges of advanced technology into universities, including Bath and Surrey.

Universities are financed mainly from Treasury funds, although all have private sources of income as well, the older universities being very wealthy. Despite this financial dependence, those who run universities have a great deal of autonomy in terms of what they teach and how it is assessed, and also in selecting undergraduates. Table 8.1 shows that their social compositions are predominantly middle-class, but there is little general evidence of an element of social selection in the admissions procedure, despite the necessity to declare father's occupation on the Universities Central Council for Admissions

Table 8.1. *Social origins of students: percentage of students whose fathers have manual occupations*

Colleges of education	40	Cambridge University	9
Full-time further education	38	Oxford University	13
Part-time further education	58	London University	21
All universities	25	Other English universities	31

Source. Derived from the Robbins Report, App. 2 (B), Tables 6, 81, 135 and C2.

application form. Suitably qualified young people from working-class backgrounds tend not to continue with their education after the sixth form, or prefer to go to other institutions of higher education, particularly if this allows them to be home-based (Couper, 1965). Tables 7.1 and 8.1 show Oxford and Cambridge have the biggest proportions of middle-class students, particularly from public schools, a result of the special relationships between these socially elite institutions (see chapter 7).

In many ways Oxford and Cambridge are the public schools of higher education, retaining a strong adherence to the ideology of the education of the cultivated man, which relates to the gentlemanly ideal of the schools. There are also resemblances to the schools' boarding element in the constituent colleges, which are the basic units of residence and teaching, and are the expression of the ideology of the university as an *academic community*, concerned not only with the instrumental transmission of knowledge, but also, perhaps more importantly, with the expressive process of the development of qualities of character, the concept of the 'whole man'.

Although several of the new universities have some mock-Oxbridge organisational features (colleges, high table, and chapel), most other universities emphasise the concept of the specialist man, reflected in strong departmental structures. They are the main educators of the major professions; Perkin (1969) has called university teaching the key profession. For some ex-public school students university education is a symbol and confirmation of their status. The orientation of others is more calculative, going to university is valued as the entry to high status occupations, although Kelsall has shown that graduates from working and lower middle-class backgrounds do not enter quite such high status jobs as others, keeping class of degree constant (Kelsall *et al*, 1970, 1972).

The student's experience of university is to some extent an extension of the experience of school. Middle-class students seem most likely to become completely involved in all aspects of university life, both social and academic. Those from lower middle and working-class homes may also embrace university life in the same way, but the research of Abbott (1971), and Box and Ford (1967) show that estranged from their families and neighbourhood by the changes their education has brought in them, they may feel themselves to be *marginal*; no longer accepted by their working-class group of origin, and unwilling to accept the middle-class group they seem destined to enter. Thus they may prefer to live at home or in lodgings rather than in colleges or halls of residence. They may try to make going to university appear as much like having a job as possible, by referring to 'going to work', leaving in the morning at the same time as their fathers and returning at the same time every evening. These attempts to escape their crisis of identity ('Who am I?'), by conscious reassociation with their family and neighbourhood, may run to avoiding all university social activities, such as dances, and taking a non-university girl friend. The Robbins Report revealed a significant tendency for working-class students to choose science subjects. This may be because these subjects form clear routes to fairly specific occupations. Box and Ford suggest that this choice may also be related to their perceiving science as a way of life and an alternative to the predominantly middle-class life styles associated with the occupations taken up by graduates entering administration and industry.

The universities are important in relation to the rest of the educational system. University teachers, especially professors, define what counts as high status academic knowledge and create new knowledge through research. Their definitions are accepted in the secondary schools through the GCE examinations that they control, and where the largest proportion of university graduates work, as teachers. Graduates also occupy many of the high status and powerful positions in industry, commerce, the civil service and politics, as well as the professions. In some cases there is a fit between the undergraduate studies and the job, as in the sciences, engineering and medicine, but this is not so in the case of the employment of many arts graduates. The successful completion of a degree for example, in history, is often thought to indicate the possession of desirable qualities valued independently of the knowledge of history gained. This illustrates a general point about qualifications gained by examinations; they have aspects of both achievement and ascription. Passing an examination is clearly an achievement, but the successful candidate does not have to go on demonstrating his qualities or knowledge by further achievement. Instead, certain qualities and attributes of knowledge are ascribed to him, often for many years after the examinations were taken. For example, when new cabinet ministers are appointed significance is often placed on whether they have a degree or not, and if they have a degree, what class of degree. The meaning of a First persists for a lifetime and may even be included in an obituary. Graduates are an educational class, with strong social class linkages.

Colleges of education

Colleges of education are the most precarious of the institutions of higher education. The oldest foundations have their origins in the teacher-training colleges set up in the mid-nineteenth century by the Churches to supplement and eventually to replace the pupil-teacher system (Taylor, 1969). They later trained teachers for the elementary schools set up after the 1870 Education Act and also provided an upward mobility route for working-class boys and girls. As Table 8.1 shows they are still more working-class in social composition than the universities.

There were nearly 200 'teacher training colleges' in 1960, most of them financed by LEAs and some by the Churches, who share their control with the DES and the universities through their Institutes of Education. Following the recommendations of the Robbins Report (1963) they were given their present name and allowed to present students for the four-year Bachelor of Education degree, as well as the three-year Certificate in Education, both validated by universities. In response to DES forecasts of teacher shortage the colleges doubled their overall numbers, training the children of the first bulge to teach those of the second. The persisting low birth rate has led to official calculations indicating a reduction in teacher supply, keeping present pupil–teacher ratios constant. These calculations have been disputed, but the consequence has been the closure of some colleges. Others, prompted by the DES, have become parts of polytechnics or incorporated by universities. A few are going it alone, introducing new non-teaching courses and broadening from being monotechnics to become *colleges of higher education*.

The pre-Robbins colleges were small, mainly single-sex, and organised around a community concept and the mother-hen principle of a close relationship between tutor and a small group of students. William Taylor (1969) analysed the underlying values:

> . . . a suspicion of the intellect and the intellectual; a lack of interest in political and structural change; a stress upon the intuitive and the intangible, upon spontaneity and creativity; an attempt to find personal autonomy through the arts; a hunger for the satisfactions of inter-personal life within the community and small group, and a flight from rationality.

The post-Robbins expansion led to many changes, as in the college described by Shipman (1967), including a decline of the community ideal. These, in retrospect, probably seem not unpleasant to those facing the current changes.

Colleges of further education

Since the White Paper of 1966 the name of technical college or college of further education has been mainly applied to the local and area colleges which provide courses below degree level.

The further education tradition in England is based on two principles: *voluntarism* and *consumerism* (King, 1976). In the nineteenth century the earliest agencies for the education of adults outside the universities were the voluntary foundations of pioneers such as Hodgkinson and Birbeck. Later, local authorities and industrial firms set up their own colleges and in-stitutions. The basis for the present provision of further educa-tion by local authorities is the 1944 Education Act which laid upon them the duty of securing 'the provision for their area of adequate facilities for further education', defined as full- and part-time education for persons over compulsory school age and 'leisure-time occupations'. This obligation does limit the volun-tary nature of the provision, but the extent varies greatly from one local authority to another. This is partly explained by the pooling system of finance to which authorities contribute accor-ding to a set formula based on the school population and the rateable value of the property in the area. Authorities can therefore put on courses, subject to the approval of the regional Advisory Council, without having to bear the full cost of the enterprise.

Voluntarism of provision is matched by voluntarism of atten-dance. The early Mechanics Institutes attracted audiences of ar-tisans for lectures on scientific and political subjects (they later attracted the middle classes for more recreational and popular courses). This was the institutionalisation of the Samuel Smiles spirit of self help. The ambitious working classes used the emerg-ing system of further education as a way of improving their career chances. In this century promotion in many industries has become related to the successful completion of courses leading to awards (Cotgrove, 1958).

A strong link exists between voluntarism and consumerism in

further education. When students choose to attend, and local firms may choose to release workers to attend, then the attractiveness of the courses becomes important. The orientation towards their consumers is expressed in the entrepreneurial character of much of the work of college principals and heads of departments, sounding out local demands and matching them with proposed courses, and as Beryl Tipton (1973) has pointed out, stimulating and shaping demands by their committee activities and by advertising.

The evolution of further education is strongly linked to the parallel emergence of the maintained system of secondary education. The use of public schools as models for the new grammar schools was associated with a lack of interest and even disapproval of anything specifically vocational in their curriculum. This apathy towards technical education was shared by industrialists, despite a succession of government reports and papers reiterating the thesis of technical education as the basis for industrial expansion. A solution was attempted in the Industrial Training Act of 1964, which empowered the Ministry of Labour to set up Industrial Training Boards for each major industry, under a Central Training Council. The Boards contain representatives of employers, trade unions, nationalised industries and educationalists, and are obliged to impose a levy on employers. Grants are paid to those who arrange for their employees to receive training approved by the Board. Thus a firm sponsoring many employees stands to gain financially.

Further education colleges provide a wide range of courses, both full and part-time, vocational (Ordinary National Diplomas, Royal Society of Arts) and academic (O and A level). They are organised on departmental lines, commonly engineering, construction, business studies and general studies. There is a strong stress on instrumental activities, useful skills and knowledge, and less on the expressive, shown in the light control of student behaviour (although those on vocational courses do have to learn the behaviour appropriate to the job, often in a work simulation, as with catering students waiting in the college restaurant). It is this aspect of the colleges that has attracted many young people from schools in recent years. The evidence of mild discontent among older pupils with the way they are treated in schools is quite strong. Given the opportunity many find refuge in the local 'tech'. King (1976) has shown these include refugees from independent schools and ex-secondary modern pupils whose schools did not provide advanced courses.

Polytechnics

The thirty regional polytechnics were created from the higher status technical colleges following the recommendations of the White Paper of 1966. They are financed by LEAs and central grants, and award degrees of the Council for National Academic Awards.

Colleges devise their own syllabuses, admission standards, and examine their own students together with external examiners. The CNAA must approve all these processes, and acts as a guardian of standards and comparability. Both the college facilities and the teaching staff must reach acceptable standards for degree level work. In addition, the Regional Advisory Council must first decide whether the degree is needed in the region. Those who run polytechnics therefore have less autonomy than those in universities, but as part of the further education tradition their directors and heads of department are entrepreneurs as well as academics. They advertise their courses; the universities, secure in the knowledge of their higher status and attractiveness to students, do not.

Consumerism has led the polytechnics to provide courses in the arts and social sciences, both of which have expanded in the universities – the so called 'swing to the arts' or 'science shortfall'. Unlike the universities they do not follow the community model, fewer students are in residence, and they do not propagate the 'cultivated' or 'whole man' image, but stress the importance of practical and useful knowledge, for example, degrees in photography and ceramics. The smaller quantity of research pursued is of an applied kind.

Under central direction the polytechnics are entering into closer association with the surviving and transformed colleges of education. (Their principal unions, respectively, the Association of Teachers in Technical Institutions [ACTI] and the Association of Teachers in Colleges and Departments of Education [ATCDE], merged in 1975 to form the National Association of Teachers in Further and Higher Education.) Together they form one-half of the *binary system* of higher education, completed by the universities. The contrast is between a tightly controlled lower status sector, and a fairly autonomous higher status one.

The open university

The idea of the Open University started life as a part of the Labour Party's 1964 election campaign, as the University of the Air. It opened in 1971 and uses radio, television, correspondence courses and study centres to bring degree level courses to adults who were denied or missed the opportunity when they were young. Together with technical colleges it provides an alternative route or second chance with respect to educational success.

Teachers and teaching 9

There are about half a million teachers in this country, forming one of the largest occupational groups. The one thing they have in common is that they all teach, but, as may be expected simply from the numbers involved, they are also quite diverse. They vary in their social characteristics, their associations, the institutions they teach in, what and how they teach.

Teachers' social characteristics

Teachers in maintained schools became teachers by virtue of their qualifications; they are either holders of certificates in education obtained from colleges of education (about two-thirds of teachers), or degree holders, who in recent times have had to take a postgraduate certificate in education at a university, college of education or polytechnic. Until the advent of comprehensive schools, most, as 'successes' of the educational system, would have come from grammar or independent schools.

Teacher training is one of the traditional routes of social mobility (see chapter 1) and a large proportion of teachers are from working-class backgrounds, but as Table 9.1 shows, these are more likely to be found in the lower status modern schools, where, until recently, most working-class children were educated. The studies of Kalton (1966) and Perkin (1967) show that the social origins of teachers in public schools and universities are more middle-class than those in maintained schools, and they are more often ex-pupils of independent schools; once again, a social fit between teacher and taught. This relationship

Teachers and teaching

Table 9.1 *Social origins of teachers* (percentages)

Father's occupation		Primary	Secondary modern	Maintained grammar
Professional	Men	6	8	13
Administrative	Women	9	11	18
Intermediate	Men	48	46	55
	Women	52	55	63
Manual	Men	46	47	32
	Women	39	34	19

Source: Adapted from Table II, 'Recruitment to teaching', by J. E. Flaid and W. Scott, in, *Education, Economy and Society,* ed. by A. H. Halsey *et al.,* 1961

is, at least in part, a reflection of social class differences in access to higher education. Colleges of education have a larger proportion of students from working-class backgrounds (Table 8.1), and these may take certificates in education which tend to lead to employment in primary and modern schools. There is also evidence from the studies of Kelsall (1970) to suggest that teaching attracts graduates from working-class backgrounds more than other available occupations. This may be partly because it is one of the few middle-class occupations that they know much about.

There is variation in the social status of different kinds of teacher; in general the higher the status of the institution the higher the status of the teacher. The Registrar General places university teachers in Social Class I (professional and managerial), but other teachers in Social Class II (intermediate non-manual). The Hall-Jones scale was based upon the ratings of different occupations by a sample of the public. University teachers and the heads of grammar schools were placed in Class 1 (professional and higher administrative), grammar school teachers and the heads of other schools in Class 2 (managerial and executive), and other teachers, the majority, in Class 3 (inspectorial, supervisory and other non-manual), together with commercial travellers and dog-breeders.

111

Education

Teachers' careers

The new entrant to teaching in a British school becomes a fully operational teacher from the start of his career. He is given the same work load as other more experienced teachers (even if he is kept away from the top stream). Thus the big transition in a teacher's career is at the point of entry, and for some it can be a trying, even harrowing, experience. Within the school system a teacher may gain promotion by obtaining a scale post or becoming a head of department or deputy head-teacher. These posts may refer either to instrumental responsibilities, such as, the head of a subject department, or to expressive responsibilities, heads of houses, tutors and counsellors. The study of Mays *et al* (1968) suggests that graduates go for the former, non-graduates for the latter. The range and number of these posts in secondary schools are tending to increase as the reorganisation leads to larger schools.

To a large extent the teacher's career prospects stem from his initial qualifications, the possession of a degree being a considerable advantage, although the growth of in-service courses and enrolment with the Open University may modify this. Within the school system the career apex is a headship where graduates are favoured. Men have a distinct advantage over women, who are generally confined to headships of girls' and infants' schools. The number of single-sex secondary schools is declining as reorganisation proceeds, so that the career chances of women teachers are not likely to improve. Indeed, the increase in size of secondary schools is partly due to a reduction in the number of schools as some amalgamate, so that there is a decline in the number of head-teacher posts.

In chapter 5 teachers were shown to act as bureaucrats in relation to the bureaucratic activities of the school. The teacher's career shows many of the features of the career of Weber's ideal-type bureaucrat (Weber, 1970). They are appointed to their positions, not elected or nominated. Their appointment is dependent on the possession of specialised qualifications.

112

Promotion is gained by superior qualifications and/or long service. The career is full-time, lifelong and pensionable.

There are career possibilities for teachers outside school teaching. Teaching experience is a part qualification for posts in educational administration, the inspectorate, for lectureships in colleges, departments and schools of education. (Most professors of education were once school teachers.) A new career possibility has been offered as wardens of LEA teachers' centres.

The existence of a national system of salaries means that teachers may pursue their careers by moving from school to school and LEA to LEA, although the study by Grace (1973, ch. 4) found that some teachers reported conflict between their loyalty to the school (part of the community ideology, see chapter 5) and their desire to move for promotion. Duggan and Stewart (1970) found that many teachers, especially non-graduates, try to get promotion appointments in the area where they went to school.

Teachers' unions and politics

The diversity of teachers is matched by a diversity of unions and associations. The Association of University Teachers and the National Association of Teachers in Further and Higher Education (an amalgam of the ATTI and ACTDE following the recent changes in colleges of education, see chapter 8) are the principal unions of higher education. The National Union of Teachers is the largest of the school teachers' unions, followed by the more militant National Association of Schoolmasters with the Union of Women Teachers. All the above-mentioned are affiliated to the Trades Union Council, an indication of the growing collectivism among the middle classes; sticking together for mutual benefit was a traditional working-class attribute. The smaller, more conservative, associations for headmasters, headmistresses, assistant masters and assistant mistresses constitute the Joint Four, after acting in concert. In addition, there are numerous associations representing special interests such as the Association of Teachers of German and the Humanist Teachers' Association. No teacher is compelled to join any union or association and may belong to more than one.

Teachers' unions act in their members' interest. The argument is frequently made that what is good for teachers is also good for their pupils (the reverse argument is seldom heard). This drawing on child-centred sentiments effectively prevents rival unions publically imputing one another's motives. One of their most important activities concerns salaries. Teachers' unions have representatives on the Burnham Committee, which establishes teachers' salary scales, together with representatives of their paymasters the LEAs and the DES, partly representing the Treasury interest. Although teachers have a measure of autonomy in their classrooms and heads in their schools, they do not have power in relation to many aspects of education that concern them. These include the official definition of a qualified teacher, teacher supply and training, the reorganisation of secondary education and some external examinations. Coates (1970) has described the ways in which teachers' unions, acting as interest groups, try to exert pressure. These include informal, regular access to the officials of the DES, formal deputations and memoranda, through memberships of central and LEA committees and the Schools Council, by giving evidence to Central Advisory Committees, and through their sponsored Members of Parliament.

The largest of the unions, the NUT, has been studied most. Originally the Nation Union of Elementary School Teachers, it draws its members from all types of school, but although most are women, men, especially head-teachers, predominate on its committees and executive. As the studies of Tropp (1957) and Manzer (1970) show, the size and diversity of membership pose problems for the executive in trying to further the interests of all its members, when some of these concern only a minority, and others may be conflicting interests. This is the problem of factionalism, the fear of a breakaway section, as happened over the issue of equal pay, leading to the formation of the NAS. The response has been to pursue policies where there is unanimity (for example, improving material conditions in schools) and those in the interest of most members, that is young, mainly women teachers (for example, improving the basic salary scale).

In these and other efforts the Union has been increasingly successful. Manzer attributes this, in part, to the long-term close relationships built up between the permanent secretaries of the Union with those of the local authorities association and of the DES. One notable 'success' concerns the Schools Council. As originally proposed by the Secretary of State in 1962 a Curriculum Study Group was envisaged as a small group of experts looking into the 'secret garden of the curriculum'. Union fears of the centralisation of the curriculum led to what was intended to be a temporary group becoming a large permanent organisation: the Schools Council. Every Committee except one has a majority of teacher union representatives. The exception is the finance committee where they are outnumbered by LEA and DES representatives, whose bodies pay the costs. This is another example of the unintended consequences of social action.

The teaching profession

The phrase 'the teaching profession' has a common usage, frequently in union activities, and the professionalisation of teaching has been the historic mission of the NUT (Tropp, 1957). There is no exact definition of a profession but there is fairly general agreement of the criteria an occupational group should meet in order to be so called. These are derived from the established professions of medicine and law, and are used as a yardstick to measure the degree of professionalisation of any aspiring occupation, as follows:

1. *A profession is based on a common body of specialist intellectual knowledge used for the benefit of the client.* The different routes to teaching mean that there is no substantial body of

specialist knowledge called education as the equivalent of medicine or law. However, now that all teachers in maintained schools must have a certificate in education, educational studies may be considered to have this status. Who is the teacher's client? The pupil? In which case clients are benefited in groups, and are not in a cash nexus with the practitioners. Perhaps their tax- and rate-paying parents are the clients to whom service is rendered?

2. *Professions have an extended period of training.* A teaching certificate is obtained after three years, a shorter time than the training of a doctor or dentist, and it has been possible to gain exemption of one year on the basis of such dubious qualifications as having been an army officer – an insight into the official concept of the teacher. However, there are no longer two-year certificate courses, and that curious anomaly the unqualified teacher officially no longer exists. The proportion of teachers with four years of higher education is increasing, and there is the long-term possibility of an all-graduate work force.

3. *Entry into the profession is controlled by its practitioners.* The definition of a qualified teacher and the rate of recruitment are governed by the DES. LEAs employ teachers and vary in the pupil–teacher ratios they maintain. Teachers' unions can only exert pressure in these matters. There have been abortive teachers' registration movements in the past (the 'Royal College of Teachers' lapsed in 1949) but they have never had the authority of law or general recognition (Parry and Parry, 1974). Teachers' wages form the largest part of the education budget, and the size of school classes is a political issue. It seems unlikely that any Secretary of State would give teachers' autonomy in this matter.

4. *Professions have a code of conduct, guaranteeing competence or recompense in the case of proven incompetence or malpractice.* Teachers' unions have codes of conduct but they are not mandatory, and only refer to relationships between colleagues, for example, no clandestine reporting of one

another to head-teachers, not to those with pupils. Within schools and in union affairs there exists what Hargreaves (1967, ch. 5) has called 'the myth of equal competence' among teachers, although private judgments are made about 'good' and 'bad' teachers. One problem is how valid judgments could be made when the tasks of teachers and the pupils they teach are so varied; compare teaching A level physics in a grammar school sixth form, with taking music and movement with the infants' reception class. Another problem is who would make such onerous and powerful judgments? Heads, advisers, pupils? However, LEAs do sometimes sack teachers and even head-teachers for incompetence, and the NUT has expelled members for sexual misdemeanours with pupils and for fascist opinions. The DES has a blacklist of teachers not to be employed in maintained schools. Someone, somewhere, is making judgments of teachers' adequacy and acceptability.

5. *Professional associations control conditions of service and freedom of practice.* Teachers in maintained schools are employed by LEAs but these lay down minimal conditions of service. More precise prescriptions may be made by head-teachers – clearly not equality among professionals. Teachers do have variable degrees of autonomy in the classroom and the opportunity to change schools without disadvantage, and so have some freedom of practice.

6. *A profession receives public recognition and commensurate high status.* As the previous section showed, school teachers are ranked below doctors and lawyers. There are a number of possible reasons for this. Firstly, there are so many teachers and they have a wide range of qualifications, in terms of both standard and specialisation. Practitioners sometimes take on the status of their clients, for example, consider the low status of probation officers. Children have a lower status than adults in British society; 'child minding' is a diatribe sometimes applied to teaching. A high proportion of teachers are women. Women receive less social status than men in British society. Virtually all the adult population has experienced of teachers

as pupils. There is little mystique. Their educational experience, often quite different from that of children today, may lead to their holding a number of unfavourable, even antagonistic stereotypes of teachers. It is possible that an unfavourable public image of teaching is projected through the fragmented structure of teachers' unions and the conflict between them. Certainly they pay little attention to public relations. Perhaps they are unsure how to answer, for example, the charge that teachers are privileged with a short working day and long holidays? The claim made by some teachers to be experts in dealing with children is made by many parents too. Some educated parents may meet their child's teacher ready to discuss Piaget and the growth of concepts. Finally, teachers may be the victims of their own success. In raising the general level of education their own educational status is relatively lowered. In developing countries teachers receive high status as an educated minority.

Etzioni (1964) has concluded that the professional yardstick is too long for teachers and introduced the concept of teaching as a *semi-profession*; a half-yard stick. Semi-professions have shorter periods of training, have less legitimate claim to authority, have a smaller body of specialised knowledge, and have less autonomy than 'true' professions. The Simpsons (1964), in an analysis of teaching in America, attribute it semi-professional status (together with social workers and medical auxiliaries) and conclude this to be a major consequence of the majority (more than 70 per cent) of teachers being women, who have a low work commitment, low demand for autonomy, and a short career orientation. The consequences are the lack of an occupational community to foster professionalism, and the use of bureaucratic rather than collegiate control in schools. The latter is generated by men who achieve positions of power in schools since success in teaching leads away from the classroom.

Is teaching in Britain better regarded as a semi-profession? Women are only just more than half of the teaching force and the teachers' unions are much more effective and powerful than the American Federation of Teachers, so that two features are conspicuously different. Whereas Anderson (1968, ch. 6) found more bureaucratic control in the form of departmental rules in American high school departments with a high proportion of women, Easthope (1975, ch. 6) found that women in English secondary schools were more estranged by the bureaucracy of big schools than were men.

A more important question is, why do teachers' unions pursue professional status? Being a 'professional' is a social cachet sought by many occupational groups, sometimes only to indicate competence, as in invitations to join the army of 'professionals', or to indicate that something is done for money and not love (the etymology of amateur), as in the oldest profession. For the teachers' unions it is an aspiration to the components of high social status; high social standing, big salaries and occupational autonomy. Sometimes they seem to be concentrating on the economic element in the belief that the others will automatically go with it; big salaries to attract the 'best' people into teaching, a contradiction of the ideal of the professional more concerned with serving others than getting money. But then, the established professions of medicine and law are not particularly good examples in this respect.

One NAS ploy in the pursuit of professionalism is extra-payment for taking out-of-school activities, and even for marking. These not only contradict the idea of the teacher as a member of the school community with a voluntary commitment to its many activities, but is also a move towards the tighter prescription of the teachers' job and a form of bureaucratisation. Most professionals do work in bureaucratic organisations (e.g., doctors in hospitals) and to some extent bureaucracy and professionalism, as traditionally conceived, are somewhat incompatable.

The NUT has long coupled the professionalisation of teaching with the idea of professional unity – a single teachers' union, based, presumably, on the NUT. In their study of medicine in

Education

America, Bucher and Strauss (1961) suggest that professions consist of a 'loose amalgamation of segments' but that a spurious unity is presented to the public to conceal internal conflicts and differences. The work force of teachers in this country is certainly a loose amalgam of segments, but there is not even a spurious unity to present to the public.

Staffroom culture

Although a small amount of team teaching is in operation, most teachers teach alone. They relate formally with colleagues through the organisation of departments and Houses, but also informally, principally in the staffroom or common room. Hargreaves (1972) has described, presumably on the basis of research, the staffroom culture in, by inference, boys' secondary schools. One norm is that of classroom autonomy in which colleagues recognise that what goes on in the classroom is a personal matter and not to be enquired about. The mediocrity norm denies the open display of effort and enthusiasm, and is strongly related to the cynicism norm. An anti-intellectualism prevents the discussion of most educational issues. There is a well-developed loyalty to the staff group relative to the head-teacher.

Hargreaves also reports that much of the staffroom conversation is about the pupils, both individuals and whole classes, which leads to a consensus view of them, and which may influence teachers before they actually encounter particular pupils or classes. King, in a study of three infant schools (unpublished), found that the children were a main topic of staffroom conversations, particularly in the schools serving the more working class areas. There was only a little evidence of the mediocrity or cynicism norms. Infant teachers are secure in their ideology and so there was little talk about educational issues, but some about techniques, for example, something new to do with an egg-box.

There is a little in the research literature about staffrooms in other kinds of school. King (1973, ch. 10) found that although mixed secondary schools generally had fewer rules controlling pupil behaviour than single-sex schools, there were more preventing pupil access to the staffroom. Presumably there were things going on in there that the teachers did not want observed. It is likely that the formal status system is expressed in staffroom relationships. The deputy head, the man-in-the-middle between head and teachers according to Burnham (1968), does much of his sounding out of colleagues there. Informal status may lead to particular chairs becoming personal property, usually those by the fire.

Teachers' teaching

There are about a third of a million classrooms in this country, but more is known about teachers' activities outside than inside them. There are two related reasons for this. Firstly, the understandable reluctance of some teachers to be observed on the job; secondly, the problems involved in making such observations (Robinson, 1974). One kind of research does not actually get inside the classroom but asks questions of teachers about their aims or objectives. These can be at such a high level of generality as to be only remotely related to classroom practice. Answers given in research situations are likely to include an element of what ought to be, and less of what actually happens.

Some researchers have got through the classroom door, but only to set up their tape or video-recorders, film cameras or closed circuit television (Channon and Delamont, 1975). These are artifacts in the situation and may distort it in unknowable ways. It may be possible to study pupils without their knowing it, but ethics demand the teacher should know. If the observer stays in the classroom he too is an artifact. Hargreaves (1967) found that when he observed in the classrooms of a secondary modern school some teachers put on a special show for his benefit or deferred their usual caning punishments until he left the room. But, however useful audio and visual recordings are as aids, a skilled observer can see and hear more; machines are incapable of inter-preting and understanding what goes on.

However, sometimes the observer fails to see the wood for the trees, and sits recording at precise time intervals tiny items of in-dividual behaviour: every smile, nod, frown or word of disap-proval. This method permits the seeing and hearing of things that have been decided in advance, but makes it difficult to grasp the flow of action and does not necessarily explain what happens. Alternatively the observer can try to be open to everything that goes on. This seemingly rather unscientific ap-proach is qualitative rather than quantitative as is best shown in the work of the American anthropologist Jules Henry (1966, chs 7, 8).

The number of variables that may affect what goes on in classrooms is enormous. Teachers vary in age, sex, education, social background, experience and ideology (progressive or traditional in the junior school). Their pupils vary in age, sex and social origins; a school class may be mixed in all these respects. In addition, the subject and the way it is taught and learnt are highly variable. The studies outlined in the following section in-dicate that there are many ways of being a teacher, and that generalisations about 'the teacher's role' are not very useful.

Studies made outside the classroom suggest that older teachers stress learning more than discipline compared with younger ones, a reflection of the difficulties of beginners, and the way that order is a prerequisite of learning (McIntyre *et al*, 1966). The Plowden Report (1967) showed that women in junior schools are less in favour of corporal punishment than men. The ideological differences among junior school teachers which seem to have classroom consequences were mentioned in the dis-cussion of the streaming/non-streaming, and the traditional/progressive controversies in chapter 6. Sara Dela-mont (1976) used direct observations in secondary schools and found differences by subjects taught. History teachers talked most, French teachers least. There were subject differences in teachers' responses to questions and in the pupils' initiatives in taking part in the lesson, and also differences in the way the same subject may be taught. Wilkinson has suggested a typology of English teachers, including, teacher as Grendel's mother acting as a guardian of literary heritage, teacher as Sigmund Freud using written work as a means of releasing (or exacerbating?) conflict and tension, teacher as group psychotherapist using drama as therapy, and finally, teacher as printer's reader regarding written work as a proof to be corrected (Wilkinson, 1966). Mention of King's unpublished observations of infant teachers was made in chapter 5, showing that the oblique methods of social control they used were based on their assumption of the innocence of their young pupils, as was, in part, their professional equanimity and pleasantness.

The influence that pupils' social origins may have on classroom relations was discussed in chapter 2, when caution was expressed about the assumption of self-fulfilling prophecy at work leading to working class failure. Hargreaves and his associates (1975) made observations in the classrooms of two mixed secondary modern schools, and found that girls seldom broke the rules of behaviour generated by individual teachers. King's observations in mixed-age infant classrooms showed that teachers distinguished between older and younger pupils in the control of their work and behaviour. What might be defined as useful play for a five-year-old was wasting time for a six-year-old.

Teachers view the control they have over their pupils as tenuous, even mysterious. When someone is able to keep order at the very beginning of their career they are often regarded as 'born teachers' with the 'gift' of special qualities. For most, acceptable levels of control come more slowly, but in retrospect is difficult to account for the quietness which has succeeded the noise. How is it done? Tutors in colleges of education seem unwilling or unable to pass on the techniques required. King found infant teachers subscribed to weather theories in explaining children's classroom behaviour, for example, windy days made them excitable.

Some studies have begun to examine the basis of social control in classrooms. Hargreaves and his associates (1975) delineated all the rules used. Apart from the school rules (well described by King, 1973), many were personal idiosyncratic rules, used to control talk, movement, time, teacher–pupil and pupil–pupil relationships. They show how the same words can have different meanings in different contexts. An example of the use of highly condensed situational meanings is given by Walker and Adelman (1976), in which the word 'strawberries' was used by a teacher in his assessment of written work. The pupils took its meaning from the teacher's favourite expression: 'Like strawberries – good as far as it goes, but it doesn't last nearly long enough.'

Some of the techniques King observed infant teachers using have been described earlier and in chapter 5. Three other methods, used to the teachers' satisfaction, can be also mentioned. The use of *eye-scanning* and *contact*, 'keeping an eye on them', involves reciprocal eye contact with pupils. The use of a *public voice*, one that, although not necessarily loud, can be heard by everyone. When a pupil is praised using this voice the praised work and behaviour is brought to everyone's attention and is frequently copied. An effective combination is that of making expectations explicit and expressing approval of the pupils meeting those expectations. Disapproval of not meeting them was less effective.

Techniques used by other teachers have been observed as follows. *Reference control* where some external authority is evoked included head-teachers and parents. The external exam or examiner may be posed as an enemy who can only be beaten by the pupils doing as teacher tells them. Another kind of reference control is based on the identities of the pupils. These are *age-reference control* (teacher to fifth year: 'All right now. Stop behaving like a set of silly first years'); *sex-reference* ('Come on boys, don't let the girls do all the work'); and *ability – status reference* ('I thought this was 2A not 2D'). (Some of these forms of control are dealt with King, 1973, ch. 10.)

Shame is the exposure of failure ('Who got ten out of ten? nine? eight? seven? six? five or less? Stand up the others'). *Guilt* poses individual blame ('You've done better work than this'). *Humour* may be used in the form of jokes, banter, irony and sarcasm (disliked by the pupils), which may shade into ridicule and verbal abuse ('noisy little git') (Hargreaves *et al*, 1975). *Threats* and *physical punishments* may be used in similar circumstances to *appeals* and *bribery*. *Symbolic rewards* such as gold stars and Smarties are common in primary schools. Waller (1932) suggested that teachers exercise control by attention to detail, such as pencil inspections.

This rather draconian analysis suggests that pupils are the powerless recipients of the teacher's orders. However, the teacher–pupil relationship is a dynamic one in which control of the classroom situation must be negotiated or bargained for. Waller suggested the principle involved was that of 'least interest'. The teacher exercises effective control by arranging that the pupils feel it is in their interests to behave themselves and work hard. What have been described are some of the ways this may be achieved.

Teachers not only attempt to control their pupils' behaviour but also what they learn; they define what counts as valid educational knowledge. In the social studies lesson observed by Keddie (1971) the teacher did not respond to the pupils 'commonsense' knowledge of the family but confined the lesson to aspects of the family prescribed by the work cards.

Teachers not only have expectations of their pupils, but pupils also have expectations of their teachers. Musgrove and Taylor, (1969, ch. 2) show that they prefer teachers who make things clear and control the class in a firm but fair manner. (British children have a well developed sense of fairness.) They are less concerned that teachers are friendly or nice-looking. Sometimes these expectations are only revealed when they are not met, and control becomes a problem for the teacher.

If education is a process of cultural transmission then this occurs not only through the content of what is taught and learnt, but also, it is thought, through the method used in the teaching–learning process. Sometimes the method may be valued above the content, as in discovery methods, where the pupil finding out for himself or herself is more important than what he or she finds out. Different teaching methods involve different kinds of relationship in the classroom which may have later consequences. Some pupils may begin to learn the ethic of science through their science lessons. King (1969) found sixth-form scientists more trusting of scientific laws, textbooks and teachers than arts specialists. Teachers are probably important role models in the formation of these subject allegiances. Dale (1966) found that many student teachers used a favourite teacher from their school days as a model or example to be followed. Carter (1966) has suggested that the working class pupils' experience of the C stream in the modern school may confirm their class values and acceptance of its life-style. He suggested that the boredom of uninteresting, repetitive work in the classroom, and the escape from this boredom in mild collective action against the teacher's authority, can be seen as a socialisation for the factory, where the work is uninteresting and repetitive, and where managerial authority is regarded with suspicion and mistrust.

Head-teachers

These powerful persons have been mentioned in previous sections and chapters; the consonance of their autonomy with the concept of the school as an individual community, and the ritualisation of their authority in the school assembly, were dealt with in chapter 5, as were their ideologies (shared with teachers), which are made operational in the organisational structures of schools, and for which in maintained schools they are legally responsible, together with discipline. The predominance of men and degree holders among head-teachers was mentioned earlier in this chapter. In line with expectation, Bernbaum (1974) has shown a slight association between the status of secondary schools and the social origins of their headmasters; less from the middle classes in modern schools. Rather unexpectedly their social origins were slightly less middle-class than those of male teachers in general.

The subordinates to the head-teacher's power are the teachers, the pupils and even their parents. They play a decisive part in the appointment and dismissal of teachers, control their careers through the distribution of scale posts and testimonials. Their power over pupils, legitmised by the principle of *in loco parentis*, is potentially great, controlling the length of their hair, where they may whistle or walk, and the content of testimonials. Head-teachers have the power to allow or prevent parents entering the school. School uniform constrains parents' choice of their own children's clothing (King, 1968).

There are limitations to this power. As was pointed out in chapter 1, there have been pupil strikes, and parents can and do remove their children from school. Governors (managers in primary schools) have dismissed head-teachers, although, in general they are not powerful bodies in maintained schools (Baron and Howell, 1974). Head-teachers like to see themselves as leaders of the school community. But leaders have a voluntary relationship with their followers. The pupils are mainly in an involuntary power relationship, which is sanctioned by law. The romantic desire to be thought of as leaders with charisma is a characteristic of those who have organisational power in this country; perhaps it is a residue of the Victorian public schools' education for leadership.

Trends and current problems 10

There are many difficulties in trying to review trends and current problems in education. The educational process is large-scale and complex, and attracts the interest of many individuals and groups, who define different things as problems and bring different ideas to the dialogue about the nature and purpose of education. Burton Clark (1962, p. 10) observed: 'never run after a bus, a woman or an educational theory – another will be along soon.' Whatever its truth with respect to the first two mentioned, it is clear that education buzzes with ephemeral fads and fashions. Deschooling and lateral thinking may go the way of callisthenics and SPERTT (the Society for the Promotion of Educational Reform through Teacher Training). Discussion here will concentrate on substantive changes in education, and on officially defined problems.

Equality in education

The modern world is sometimes considered to have started with the French Revolution. The ideas of freedom, equality, and, to a lesser extent, fraternity, have become part of political processes, including those of education. Equality in education has been one of the most important ideas of this century; an idea with many facets, and with many consequences in terms of change and policies, but not accepted by all.

Equality is held by some as an ideal in education. Inequalities may exist between individuals, institutions (schools or types of school) or between social groups, including the social classes, ethnic groups or the sexes. In this chapter attention is concentrated first on social class; ethnic and sexual inequalities are discussed later. The inequalities may be of different things: educational provision, opportunities, esteem or attainment. Much of the confusion in the discussion of equality in education is that it is not always made clear who the inequalities are between and of what the inequalities consist. It should be noted that equality of anything between individuals, institutions or groups does not make them the same. The Tiller Girls show equality of height, but they are all different individual girls. If the borough surveyor were paid as much as the refuse collector they would still be doing different jobs. Different inequalities in education have been officially defined as problems, which have in some cases led to policies designed to move towards the goal or ideal of equality.

Equality of provision between individuals is attempted in the provision of free meals, clothing and financial assistance for children whose deficiencies in these things are judged to impair their response to education. A similar principle is involved in the sliding scale of higher education grants by parents' income. These policies are based on the *differential income theory* of the relationship between educational attainment and family income (see chapter 2).

The most important example concerns inequalities between schools; the *Educational Priority Area* (EPA) concept, invented by the Plowden Committee (1967; the programme of EPA action–research is reported in Halsey, 1972-75). The Committee failed to grasp the nettle of social class differences in education, despite their demonstration in commissioned surveys. Instead they located the 'problem' of working class failure in the schools of EPAs, defined according to a number of criteria concerning the school and its catchment area; the proportion of children with free meals, from large or incomplete families, showing poor attendance or truancy, defined as retarded, disturbed or handicapped, and unable to speak English, from overcrowded homes with low rateable values. These are schools in urban areas with large proportions of children from poor, lower-working class homes. Bernstein and Davies (1969) have pointed out that the Plowden Committee assumed that all the schools in an EPA needed help, and did not enquire whether some were more successful than others, using their own criteria of the 'good' primary school outlined in the Report.

Many of these schools had poor material facilities, and as a consequence of the committee's recommendation more money has been made available for improvements. In some cases this has not only been to bring the school up to the standards of others but to give them more and better facilities. This is the principle of *positive discrimination* which attempts to achieve not just equality of provision between schools, but inequalities favouring those felt most in need. The Committee hoped that this would help to reduce inequalities of educational outcome by the improvement of the children's attainment. This is based on the *differential provision theory* (chapter 2).

Coleman (1966) and Jencks *et al* (1973) in their surveys of American education found social class inequalities of provision, but claimed that these did not contribute substantially to social class differences in attainment. Byrne *et al* (1975) refute this, using British data, but King (1974, 1976, ch. 6) has shown that even when an LEA had made better provision in the schools serving working-class areas, the levels of attainment in such schools were lower than those in middle-class areas (see chapter 2). It must be concluded that *existing* differences in provision (which are not large) make little difference to attainment, but it is possible that a large measure of positive discrimination may be effective, possibly over a long period of time. Two other important points may be made. Teachers are concerned with more than the teaching of basic skills and helping pupils pass exams, important though these are. The generous provision of staff and pleasant surroundings may be valued for their contribution to the quality of relationships in school. The payment of salary supplements to because their culture is discontinuous with that of the school and may be in conflict with it. The argument is stood on its head; teachers fail working-class children because the culture of the school is in conflict with that of the children. This is an attempt to shift the 'blame' for failure away from the child (the 'individualisation of failure') and his family, and put it on to the educational system in general and teachers in particular.

The suggested educational implication is that some of the elements of working-class culture should be incorporated in the curriculum and teaching styles used with working-class children. (There have been no explicit suggestions of an education based totally on working class culture.) This has been a part of the idea behind the *community school*. Following the Plowden Report a programme of action – research was started in six EPA's under the direction of A. H. Halsey (1972-75). The community school has been applied in these areas, and is perhaps best known in connection with the work of Eric Midwinter (1972) in Liverpool. The project work of primary school children has been based on studies of the local community, and, following the suggestions of the Plowden Committee, the schools have been made more accessible to parents. The specific social class element in the programme could be seen as a new version of the Victorian view of education confirming existing class status. In Deptford the Beatty's programme has concentrated more on providing children with experiences outside the local area, such as short-term residence in country areas. An evaluation of these actions is difficult since they involve changes in the content of education and are not necessarily intended to improve measurable attainment.

An extension of the community school is the idea of *community education*, particularly associated with the Yorkshire project. Here education is not only based on the local community but attempts to involve the community. This includes 'education shops' offering advice, the display of children's work in stores, and the encouragement of mothers to form their own school playgroups, which are thought to be of benefit to

teachers in EPA schools is intended to improve morale and reduce turnover. Children are in school for a large proportion of their lives and such things as pleasant surroundings, plentiful books and indoor lavatories may be intrinsically valued, particularly if these are not to be found in their homes.

Equality of opportunity may be linked to equality of provision, but not always; money can be spent on different things. A resurfaced playground is not likely to improve attainment, and some opportunities can be created at no extra cost. Equality of opportunity between the social classes was the original idea of equality in education, particularly associated with R. H. Tawney (1952). This essentially meritocratic idea existed in embryo form in the free place system of the prewar grammar schools and in the later abolition of their fees, in the introduction of exams to modern schools, the use of technical colleges for second chances, and most explicitly in the setting up of comprehensive schools, where equality of opportunity is intended to exist from school to school (chapter 7). In each of these cases it has been shown that the more opportunities are provided the more they are taken up. This is the *gatekeeper effect*. Children officially defined or labelled as non-academic and sent to modern schools without exams did not have the opportunity to prove that definition wrong; the definition was 'real' in its consequences (Thomas, 1928). When the examination gate was opened, because of doubts about the reality of their low ability, they were permitted to try to prove the eleven-plus wrong.

The national provision of *nursery schools and classes* (attached to infant schools) for under-fives is small; less than 500. These are mainly in working-class areas. The Plowden Report showed that the proportion of children from semiskilled and unskilled workers' families receiving nursery education (often part-time) was similar to that for children of professional and managerial workers, but the latter were mainly in private establishments. The belief in the importance of the first few years of life for intellectual development led the Plowden Committee to recommend more nursery provision in EPAs. A few more were provided under the Urban Aid programme to poor areas of cities, often EPAs, and, like them, a form of positive discrimination by social area. There is little evidence of advantages of nursery education in terms of school progress, so the Plowden Committee's hope that they may contribute to equality of attainment appears a faint one (Stevenson, 1975; Woodhead, 1976). However, some children may acquire the social competences of feeding and dressing themselves, being toilet trained and recognising colours which they might otherwise not have gained at home. In addition, it has been argued that the actual experience of the nursery school is better than that which they would otherwise have had at home, at the child-minder's, or in the street.

The allocation of nursery places is an example of positive discrimination of the level of the individual child, chosen by teachers, health visitors and others as being most deserving. Individual primary school children are also sent to the day centres set up by some LEAs to provide extra teaching, often on special programmes. There is little evidence that these small amounts of extra help improve progress (Woods, 1975). As in some of the American compensatory education programmes the attempt has been to 'boost' ability. This follows the *differential ability theory*; educational failure is due to lack of ability (chapter 2). But it also assumes that ability can be acquired. The Plowden Committee demurred from defining individual educational priority children in this way for fear of social stigma.

Equality of esteem was the pious hope for the modern school in relation to the grammar school (chapter 6). Comprehensive reorganisation is removing the respective low and high esteem that went with these schools. This may be replaced by differences in esteem between comprehensive schools on the basis of their social compositions; those with more middle-class children are likely to have the better exam results and the bigger sixth forms. This is one argument against neighbourhood schools produced by zoning, and for the use of banding to give a more even distribution of the social classes in the schools (chapter 6).

The removal of the direct grant is also a move to equalise e (chapter 7).

Inequalities of esteem between types of school are a qualities of esteem between the pupils who go to schools; the 'pride' of the grammar school pupil and th of the modern school pupil. This stratification of child reduced by the use of non-streamed groups, the socia being that they remove the 'effects' produced by the of the high esteem top stream and the low est (chapters 2 and 6). The moves to combine O level be viewed as part of this kind of equality.

Equality of esteem between social groups is th concept of *cultural relativity*. The American eq EPA child have been called 'culturally deprive sociological nonsense; no one can be deprived of cept perhaps by isolation from all human conta (Culture is not just learnt once, it is re-learnt interaction with others in everyday life.) Th deprived' is an evaluative one in which the p ghetto children, usually black, is judge deficient. This is the *vacuum ideology*; th that has to be filled up with 'culture' (see this view, such as Nell Keddie (1973), su middle-class perspective, and that the cu filled up with, although sometimes calle is middle-class culture. Cultural relati of different cultures which makes no e them, but examines the qualities of they play in the lives of those who

This perspective is illustrated b such as Gladwin's (1973) descriptic of the Trukese. By extension it is a 'good' as white, and working middle-class. This is an asp Bernstein's work on language (cl the *cultural discontinuity thec* both small children and their mothers. These efforts may be called social engineering; the use of education to change local society, particularly mothers.

Many of the policies to achieve equality of provision, opportunity and esteem are seen as a means to equality of educational attainment. This is seldom used to mean equality between individuals. The notion of all children reaching the same level of attainment is antithetical to the idea of the normal distribution of ability and the operation of the examination system based on the same idea. Equality of outcome or attainment usually refers to the elimination of social class differences – the *class gap*. In some communist countries working-class students or those who have worked in manual occupations have sometimes been given preferential entry or course credits in higher education (Grant, 1964). These have not been suggested in this country, presumably because they would be considered unfair means to the end. This may also apply to quotas or credits given to schools or areas favouring the working class for exam passes or university places.

There is, however, evidence of the closing of the class gap. Little and Westergaard (1970) collated the results of a number of surveys to show that the proportion of working-class children receiving an extended education had increased. The data used referred to the period before comprehensive reorganisation and the expansion of higher education (and one with little reform of the curriculum), both of which were in part intended to further close the gap, and probably have.

The doubts and disappointments concerning the EPA project, expressed even by their director, should be set against this general background of increased working class success (Halsey, 1974). Despite the hard work and commitment of those involved, the total amount of intervention is small in amount and duration. Certainly not enough to warrant the conclusion in the title of an article by Bernstein (1970), 'Education cannot compensate for society'. In the case of the EPAs it might be said that education has not yet compensated.

135

The implication of the Bernstein thesis is that changes are necessary in society. Leaving aside calls for revolution, reforms in such things as housing provision and social security rights have occurred and can be furthered. However, the education/society dichotomy is, as was pointed out in chapter 1, a dubious one. School is a large part of the society of children. Educational reforms are social reforms for children. If there were equal provision, opportunities and esteem in education, then there would be equality in a large sector of British society. The duration of education in everyone's life permits its nature being judged intrinsically as well as extrinsically – as an experience as well as a pay-off.

Sociological studies of education sometimes produce a reaction of despair. Working-class children may be seen to be doomed to failure by a middle-class institution. However, the class gap has been closed. Many working-class children are rated as highly by their teachers and do as well in exams as middle-class ones. Many working-class parents show as much interest in their children's education as middle-class parents. Many of them, the socially aspiring, would like to be middle-class, and want their children to have the chance to be so through educational success (chapter 3). Many of them make it, often as teachers. The EPA concept was correct to the extent that it defined the 'problem' not as one concerning all working-class children, but mainly those of the poor semiskilled and unskilled workers; the 'roughs' not the 'respectables'.

Perhaps in all of this there is the educated person's high evaluation of education. It is conceivable that young people from some working-class homes, choose, as freely as choices may be considered free, to have nothing more to do with it, preferring to take up what they define as a good job, perhaps the same sort as their respected fathers before them.

Immigrants and education

It was only in the mid-1960s that the education of coloured immigrant children was officially defined as a problem. Until 1965 no national statistics were kept of the numbers of such children in schools. They now form about 3 per cent of all pupils in maintained schools. Of these most are West Indian, the rest mainly Indian and Pakistani. The majority of them are found in about one-tenth of the total number of schools, often those with pre-existing social problems and in designated EPAs. The DES stopped issuing statistics in 1973. This was partly because of difficulties in defining an immigrant child (a category that includes Prince Charles), and the discrimination required at the school level in making the statistical returns.

The official analysis of the problems that cause a 'strain' within the schools include language difficulties, problems of assessment in the absence of culture-free or culture-neutral tests, prejudice and hostility on the part of the teachers and indigenous pupils, and the fears of lowered standards on the part of teachers and indigenous parents. Most of these are aspects of discontinuities between the cultures of immigrant groups and that of the school. The official policy, outlined in Circular 7/65 was to disperse immigrant children to prevent the formation of predominantly immigrant schools. Only six LEAs have used this 'bussing' policy, which is unpopular with both immigrant and indigenous parents.

It is now being recognised that the culture of each of the immigrant groups exists in a particular discontinuity, and therefore each group constitutes a different kind of 'problem'. Coard (1971) has claimed that many of the high proportion of West Indian children in remedial education have been wrongly defined as lacking ability, but are sent because of the behaviour problems they present to teachers. Some immigrant children and their parents seem to lack sensitivity to the signals generated in the educational process. Most native-born children know what is implied by being in the bottom stream or going to a secondary modern school. The report by Beetham (1968) on immigrant school leavers in Birmingham showed that many had unrealistic career ambitions. The survey also showed that the rate of voluntary staying on was higher for immigrant than non-immigrant pupils. This and other evidence suggests that immigrants may place a high value on education, especially in the way that educational success permits access to non-manual occupations. A study by Durojaiye (1971) suggested that the cultural patterns of Indian and Pakistani families are similar to those of the home-centred, aspiring working class, which many educationally successful working-class children come from. The study by Taylor (1973) in Newcastle upon Tyne showed that both Indian and Pakistani pupils did better at school and stayed on into the sixth form more often than 'English' boys in the same school. Clearly not all immigrant children cause 'strain' or constitute problems.

Assuming that the current immigration laws remain, some of the problems will be self-extinguishing. It remains to be seen whether any of the immigrant groups will adopt the Catholic solution and create their own school system, or adopt the Jewish solution in keeping their children mainly within the maintained sector of education, using the family and religious institutions for the transmission of their traditional culture, so adding to the many ways of being British.

Sexual inequality in education

The growth of political consciousness among women has recently been associated with concern about sex-differences in education. Table 10.1 shows it is possible to refer to a *sex-gap* in attainment, which widens as the level of education rises (King, 1971).

Is it possible to account for the sex gap using similar theories to those used for the class gap (chapter 2)? A sex differential ability theory would propose that girls are less academically able than boys. However, longitudinal studies of children have shown that girls tend to obtain slightly higher scores than boys in ability tests, especially in the early years of schooling. There is no clear evidence of a sex differential in access to key institutions that would explain the phenomenon, and there is no clear evidence

Table 10.1 *The sex gap: percentage incidence of entering courses*

	Boys	Girls
O level	63.8	40.7
A level	19.1	10.6
Full-time degree	5.8	3.0

Source. Derived from *Robbins Report,* App. 1, sec. 2, Table 1, p. 38.

for a sex differential provision theory. Some evidence actually flies in the face of its basic proposition. The Crowther Report (1959, vol. 1) found that the provision for science in girls' schools was inferior to that in mixed grammar schools, but a larger proportion chose to specialise in science in the single sex schools.

A sex cultural discontinuity theory to explain differences in access would propose the existence of a specifically masculine component in the transmitted culture. In terms of the knowledge transmitted and the legitimacy of the educational process this may be partly true, but in terms of personnel the educational system is predominantly female, especially at the primary school level where 75 per cent of the teachers are women. Many studies have shown that girls receive more favourable ratings for work and behaviour from their teachers (e.g. Brandis and Bernstein, 1974). This may be explained in terms of feminine value orientations, for example, the more ready compliance with authority, which may form a part of the more conservative political orientation of women. Another theory is that girls have a stronger orientation towards marriage than towards occupations compared with boys, and this has consequences for the relevance and their evaluation of education.

The official definition of a problem of sexual inequality in education is shown in the Sex Discrimination Act of 1976 which forbids the continuation of teaching some subjects to only one sex in mixed schools.

A parallel has been drawn between the class gap and the sex gap in education. But children are not only boys and girls but

Education

also are from different social class backgrounds. Table 10.2 shows educational levels reached, analysed by sex and social class.

Table 10.2 *The sex and class gap: percentage entering courses*

	Father's occupation			
	Non-manual		Manual	
	Boys	Girls	Boys	Girls
O level	79.4	78.7	58.7	34.3
A level	38.1	28.1	12.1	4.3
Full-time degree	14.8	9.4	2.5	0.7

Source. As Table 10.1

At each level of education the sex gap is wider for the working class than for the middle class, and the class gap is bigger for girls than boys. As the level of education rises the sex gap widens for both classes, but most for the working class. The class gap also widens for both sexes, but more for girls than for boys.

It is clear that sexual inequalities in education are inextricably part of social class inequalities, and that neither should be considered separately from the other. Middle-class boys are the most advantaged, working-class girls the most disadvantaged, the former having twenty-one times more chance of taking a degree than the latter. It would be a very difficult to explain these patterns in terms of any of the theories discussed before. The difficulties arise from a lack of research in which both sex and social class have been studied. Theories are required that will not just explain class differences in education, but the different educational experiences of four basic pupil types; middle-class boys, middle-class girls, working-class boys and working-class girls.

King (1971) has tentatively suggested one based upon a distinction made by Havighurst (1961) between the symbolic value of education, where it is valued as an indicator of high social status, and the functional value, in which it is valued as a means to enter a desired occupation. Middle-class boys show a high evaluation of education for both symbolic and functional purposes; they have to maintain status and also often gain entry to occupations through certification. Working-class boys do not have status that is confirmed by the receipt of education but many gain access to desired occupations through education; they show low symbolic evaluation but possibly high functional evaluation. Middle-class girls have a high symbolic evaluation (status confirming), but a lower functional one, related to their stronger orientation to marriage. Working-class girls show a low evaluation of both the symbolic and functional; their orientation is towards early marriage, their status is not confirmed by education. The different rates of attainment may be (in part) related to these different kinds and levels of evaluation.

The curriculum

What is taught and learnt, and how it is taught and learnt, have become of greater interest and concern. In higher education the new universities introduced degrees which draw knowledge from a number of traditional disciplines, such as molecular biology, or degrees drawing on knowledge and behaviours formerly not dealt with directly, including business studies. The CNAA (Council for National Academic Awards) degrees may be taken in subjects clearly related to highly specialised technologies, such as ceramics.

Within the schools two agencies have been principally concerned with the support of curriculum reforms, the Schools Council and the Nuffield Foundation. The latter is now less important in this field than it was in the mid-1960s, when its support of science and mathematics projects in regional teachers' workshops gave rise to a new institution, now mainly supported by the LEAs, the *teachers' centre*

The early projects supported by the Schools Council were mainly concerned with preparation for the raising of the school leaving age. These include the breaking down of the subject barriers, as in the emergence of a new elastic category called the humanities, work experience schemes, visits and choices based on interest. But now the range of projects has widened to cover children of all ages, the whole of the traditional curriculum and the introduction of new elements into the curriculum, the results of which are reported in the form of working papers.

The expansion of higher education has been accompanied by proportionately more students taking arts subjects and social science. This 'swing towards the arts' or 'science shortfall' has been shown to start in the secondary school, and has caused concern because it was held that the economy required an increasing proportion of scientists and engineers. This led to a number of enquiries about scientific education. The Dainton report calls for an active policy within the schools to halt the swing from science, including making science and mathematics more attractive to pupils, and by making mathematics a compulsory sixth form subject. Similar recommendations were made for changes in higher education by the Swann Report (1968), including the 'humanisation' of science courses. Many curriculum projects in schools have concerned science, even its introduction to infants. However, the unemployment of science graduates in the early 1970s contradicts the idea of a shortage in industry, and suggests that the concern was really about the supply of science undergraduates.

The domination of the Schools Council by the teachers' unions (see chapter 9) has led to the backing of projects covering the wide range of interests of their members, so that no definite line or policy regarding the curriculum has been followed. This is an indication that fears about the centralisation of control of the curriculum have little foundation. Finally, there is little reliable evidence to show how extensive or permanent are the intended changes. Most teachers seem to be rather eclectic, taking and adapting ideas from different sources, but not always introducing totally new methods. To do so would imply that they had been doing things incorrectly in the past. Curriculum changes imply identity changes. Geography teachers may go on being geography teachers even when the timetable defines their activities as Humanities or Environmental Studies.

An overview

Education in modern Britain is large-scale, complex, and variable, and therefore difficult to summarise without overgeneralising or being banal. In his speculative essay, 'Open schools, open society?' Bernstein (1971) suggested that education was becoming more 'open'. The comprehensive and non-streaming movements are clear examples of this, but the binary policy of higher education and the separate curriculum for non-examinees in secondary schools represent closures. King (1976) has shown that within secondary schools, open organisational features, such as parents' ease of access to teachers, often exist together with closed features, such as hierarchical control by prefects. In a more sophisticated version of the theory Bernstein proposes that the basic changes are in 'educational knowledge codes', from 'collection' codes to 'integrated' ones. As with the earlier paper no empirical evidence is presented to support the thesis, and the changes occuring in education are explained in terms of changes outside, principally the industrialisation process. Doubts have already been expressed about this kind of distinction between education and society (see earlier and chapter 1).

Less abstractly and more concretely it can be suggested that education has been recently marked by three trends; *expansion, diversity*, and *centralisation*. These have been based on two important elements; *ideology* and the *economy*.

The expansion of education for the ages of compulsory schooling has been the outcome of the birth bulges and the institutionalised ideology of mass education. (A few right wing groups do want the school leaving age lowered.) The expansion of higher and further education has been fed more by the trend for young people to receive voluntarily more education in pursuit of personal ambition. Here the demand has been met by the establishment of new courses and qualifications (CSE, CNAA degrees) in a diversity of higher education institutions and forms of comprehensive school, and legitimised by a meritocratic ideology (chapters 6 and 8).

The number of interest groups has increased. Parent, pupil and student groups have been added to those of teachers and lecturers, local authorities, political parties and governments. (The pupil groups are the Schools Action Union and the National Union of School Students.) All assert ideologies related to the interests of their members, but they vary in their power to implement them. Of the established power groups governmental authority embodied in the DES has become more powerful. Its control is now felt in relation to the form of schooling, once the sole domain of the LEAs (chapter 6), and in examinations, once totally in the hands of teachers (CSE) and the universities (GCE), since any changes now require the sanction of the Secretary of State. In higher education it has created new institutions, the polytechnics and the CNAA, and has controlled the colleges of education, in some cases to the point of extinction. This tightening of central control has been felt most in maintained schools and in the so-called public sector of higher and further education. Under both Labour and Conservative governments the autonomy of the high status institutions, the public schools and universities, has not been seriously challenged.

The struggle among interest groups is also concerned with the competition for the scarce resources for education, and for the resource of education itself. The increase in the central authority's power is partly related to the stronger assertion of social and educational ideologies; principally those relating to equality by Labour, and *laissez-faire* by the Conservatives. But it is also related to a concern about the distribution and use of an enormous amount of public money.

One of the major themes of sociology concerns the human consequences of social change. In terms of scale, organisation, control and content, British education is in a state of rapid change compared with almost any other historical period. One human consequence is uncertainty, even anxiety. This is shown in the increased militance of teachers and students, in the enquiries into the effectiveness of educational methods and policies, and in the public debates about the nature and purpose of education, some of which lead to further changes in policy and practice affecting the essential educational relationships and processes in the classroom. Perhaps these are the symptoms of an educational system moving out of the long shadow of the nineteenth century, and being slowly changed from an elitist institution, where education is a privilege and where some children get more than others or receive what is thought to be a better, exclusive education, to an egalitarian consumer industry, based upon the realisation of individual aspirations, and where education is a right.

References and further reading

Reports
Published by HMSO. In date order:

Hadow Report	1926	Consultative Committee to the Board of Education, *The Education of the Adolescent.*
Spens Report	1938	Consultative Committee on Secondary Education, *Secondary Education: with special reference to grammar schools and technical high schools.*
Norwood Report	1943	Secondary Schools Examination Council, *Curriculum and Examinations in Secondary Schools*
Fleming Report	1944	*Board of Education, The Public Schools and the General Education System*
Central Advisory Council for Education*	1954	*Early Leaving.* The first of the postwar education reports incorporating survey material

* *CACs are appointed by the Secretary of State for Education; their recommendations are advisory, not mandatory.*

Crowther Report	1959–60	Central Advisory Council for Education (England), *15–18.* Vol. 2 (1960) contains the National Service Survey.
Beloe Report	1960	Secondary Schools Examination Council, *Secondary Schools Examinations other than G.C.E.*

Robbins Report	1963	*Higher Education*, report of a Committee appointed by the Prime Minister.
Newsom Report	1963	Central Advisory Council for Education (England), *Half Our Future.*
Plowden Report	1967	Central Advisory Council for Education (England), *Children and their Primary Schools*, Vol. 1 *Report*, Vol. 2, *Research and Surveys* (including the National Child Development Survey and a survey of parents of primary school children).
Public Schools Commission:	1968	Department of Education and Science, Public Schools Commission, *First Report: 2 Vols.*
Public Schools Commission	1970	*Second Report*, vol.1, *Independent Day Schools and Direct Grant Grammar Schools; 2 vols.*

Extracts from most of these reports appear in J. S. Maclure (ed.) *Educational Documents 1816–1968*, Methuen, 1969

Chapter 1 Education and society

ACE (Advisory Centre for Education) (1969) *Verdict on Facts.* 'A white paper'.

Auld, Robert (1976) *The William Tyndale Junior and Infant Schools: a report*, Greater London Council.

Bernstein, B. B. et al (1971) 'Ritual in education', in B. R. Cosin et al, eds., *School and Society*, Routledge & Kegan Paul. This is a speculative essay not based on empirical research.

Boaden, N. (1973) 'Local authorities and education', in J. Raynor and J. Harden, eds, *Equality and City Schools*, Routledge & Kegan Paul. A study of former county boroughs.

Burgess, T. (1972) *A Guide to English Schools*, Penguin. An easily readable guide to the administrative structure of education.

Campbell, F. (1956) *The Eleven Plus and All That*. Watts. A social history of London grammar schools.

Collins, R. (1972) 'Functional and conflict theories in educational stratification', in B. R. Cosin, ed., *Education, Structure and Society*, Penguin. The Weberian conflict approach advanced in this article has been followed in this section and in other parts of the book.

Cox, C. B. and *Dyson, A. E.* eds (1969) 'Fight for education', *Critical Quarterly Society, A 'black paper'*.

Crosland, A. and *Boyle, E.* (1971) *The Politics of Education*, Penguin. Transcripts of interviews with two former Secretaries of State for Education, Labour and Conservative respectively, being cautiously frank.

Cuddity, R. et al, eds (1970) *The Red Paper*, Islander.

David, M. (1973) 'Approaches in organisational change in LEAs', *Educational Administration Bulletin*, 1. One of the few pieces of research about CEOs.

The Education Committees Yearbook, Councils and Education Press. This is produced annually and contains lists of educational interest and power groups.

Esland, G. (1971) 'Teaching and learning as the organisation of knowledge', in Young, ed. (1971). This is a speculative essay drawing on secondary sources.

Floud, J. and *Scott, W.* (1961) 'Recruitment to teaching in England and Wales', in Halsey, *et al.*, (1961). A dated but still valuable survey.

Glass, D. V., ed. (1954) *Social Mobility in Britain*, Routledge & Kegan Paul. Note chapters 5 and 10 in this compilation of studies.

Halsey, A. H. et al, eds. (1961) *Education, Economy and Society*, Free Press.

Jackson, B. and *Marsden, D.* (1962) *Education and the Working Class*, Routledge & Kegan Paul. A partial but affecting study based on the careers of a small number of working class grammar school successes.

Kalton, G. (1966) *The Public Schools: a factual survey*, Longmans. Commissioned by the Headmasters' Conference but unbiased.

Kogan, M. (1975) *Educational Policy making*, Allen & Unwin. A study of educational interest groups and parliament which contains useful summaries of policies and their supporters.

King, R. A. (1968) 'The headteacher and his authority', in J. B. Allan, ed., *Headship in the 1970's*, Blackwell 1968; also in G.Fowler *et al*, eds., *Decision-making in British Education*, Heinemann, 1973. An essay both factual and speculative.

King, R. A. (1973) *School Organisation and Pupil Involvement*, Routledge & Kegan Paul. This research covered seventy-two different secondary schools and 7,000 pupils: note chapters 1 and 2.

Lacey, C. (1970) *Hightown Grammar*, Manchester University Press. A case study of a single school: note chapter 4.

Lawton, D. (1975) *Class, Culture and Curriculum*, Routledge & Kegan Paul.

Manzer, R. (1975) 'The political origins of the Schools Council', in R. Bell and W. Prescott eds., *The Schools Council: a second look*, Ward Lock.

Marshall, T. H. (1963) 'Citizenship and social class', in *Sociology at the Crossroads*, Heinemann.

Marson, D. (1973) *Children's Strikes in 1911*, History workshop Pamphlet no. 9, Ruskin College, Oxford. The slogan was 'Shorter hours and no cane!'

Martin, F. M. (1954) 'Some subjective aspects of social stratification', in Glass, ed. (1954).

Mitchell, G. D. (1964) 'Education, ideology and social change in England', in G. K. Zollschan and W. Hursch, eds., *Explorations in Social Change,* Routledge & Kegan Paul. An examination of educational changes at the end of the nineteenth

149

Education

century and early twentieth century.

Newson, J. and *Newson, E.* (1963) *Infant Care in an Urban Community*, Penguin 1965 *Newson, J.* and *Newson, E.* (1968) *Four Year Olds in an Urban Community*, Penguin, 1970 *Newson, J.* and *Newson, E.* (1976) *Seven Year Olds in the Home Environment*, Allen & Unwin, 1976. The first three reports of a longitudinal study of families in Nottingham.

Taylor, G. and *Saunders, J. B.* (1971) *The New Law of Education*, 7th edn., Butterworths. A compendium of all the current laws, regulations and recommendations.

Turner, R. H. (1961) 'Modes of ascent through education: sponsored and contest mobility', in Halsey *et al* (1961). A classic of the sociology of education, which although speculative is also acceptably imaginative.

Weber, Max. (1970) Weber's key writings are well anthologised; see for example P. Worsley, ed., *Modern Sociology*, Penguin, 1970; K. Thompson and J. Tunstall, eds, *Sociological Perspectives*, Penguin, 1971.

Woodhall, M. and *Blaug, M.* (1968) 'Productivity trends in British secondary education, *1950-63' Sociology of Education, 41.*

Young, M. (1961) *The Rise of the Meritocracy*, Penguin. This unusual novel draws on the sociological work of the time and presents a future Britain where occupations are directly linked to measured intelligence.

Young, M. F. D. (1971) 'An approach to the study of curricula as socially organised knowledge', in Young, ed (1971) A review of several approaches to the sociology of educational knowledge.

Young, M. F. D., ed. (1971) *Knowledge and Control*, Macmillan.

Young, M. F. D. (1975): 'On the politics of educational knowledge' in Bell and Prescott eds. See Manzer (1975).

Further reading

Bourdieu, P. (1973) 'Cultural reproduction and social reproduc-

150

tion', in R. Brown, ed., *Knowledge, Education and Cultural Change*, Tavistock. Translated from the French and about France, but with possible applications to this country.

Kogan, M. and *Van der Eyken, W.* (1973) *County Hall: the role of the Chief Education Officer*, Penguin. Interviews with three recently retired CEOs.

Squibb, P. G. (1973) 'The concept of intelligence', *Sociological Review, 21.*

Chapter 2 Class chances in education

Abel-Smith, B. and *Townsend, P.* (1965) *The Poor and the Poorest*, Bell. A seminal work by the 'poverty professors'.

Byrne, D. S., Williamson, W. and *Fletcher, B.* (1972) *The Poverty of Education*, Robertson. See also their article in *Sociology, 6.*

CAC (1954) *Early Leaving*: see Reports.

Campbell, F. (1954) *The Eleven Plus and All That*, Watts.

Case, P. and *Ross J. M.* (1965) 'Why do children leave school early?' *New Society, 162.* This is part of the (1964,1968) studies by Douglas.

Crowther Report (1960) *(See* Reports). Vol. 2 contains three valuable surveys.

Dale, R. R. and *Griffiths, D.* 1965 *Downstream: A study of failure in a grammar school*, Routledge & Kegan Paul.

Davies, B. (1968) *Social Needs and Local Services*, Joseph.

Douglas, J. W. B. (1964) The Home and the School, MacGibbon Kee. The third volume reporting a longitudinal study of children born in 1964.

Douglas, J. W., Ross, J. M. and *Simpson, H. R.* (1968) *All Our Future*, Davies. The sample from the Home and the School studied in the secondary school.

Ellison, T. and *Williams, W.* (1971) 'Social class and Children's reading preferences' *Readings,I*

Floud, J. E. ed, Halsey, A. H. and *Martin, F. M..* (1957) *Social*

Class and Educational Opportunity, Heinemann. A seminal study in the sociology of education, concerning Middlesbrough and south-west Hertfordshire.

Goodacre, E. (1968) *Teachers and their Pupils' Home Background*, National Foundation for Educational Research. A selection appears in B. R. Cosin *et al*, eds. *School and Society*, Routledge & Kegan Paul, 1971.

Halsey, A. H. and Gardner, L. (1953) 'Sociometric relationships between grammar school boys and girls', *British Journal of Sociology, 4.*

Hargreaves, D. H. (1967) *Social Relations in a Secondary School*, Routledge & Kegan Paul. A case study of 'Lumley' secondary modern.

Holly, D. (1965) 'Profiting from a comprehensive school', *British Journal of Sociology, 16.*

Horobin, G., et al (1967), 'The social differentiation of ability', *Sociology, 1.*

Jackson, B. (1964) *Streaming: an education system in miniature*, Routledge, & Kegan Paul. A mixture of polemic and research.

Kalton, G. (1966) *The Public Schools*, Longmans.

Keddie, N. (1971) 'Classroom knowledge', in M. F. D Young, ed., *Knowledge and Control*, Macmillan. One of the few research studies to use the phenomenological approach advocated by B. R. Cosin in the same volume.

Keddie, N. (1973) Introduction to *Tinker Tailor* ... N. Keddie, ed. Penguin.

King, R. A. (1969) *Values and Involvement in a Grammar School*, Routledge & Kegan Paul.

King, R. A. (1973) *School Organisation and Pupil Involvement*, Routledge & Kegan Paul.

King, R. A. (1974) 'Social class, educational attainment and provision', *Policy and Politics, 3.* An LEA case study.

Lacey, C. (1970) *Hightown Grammar*, Manchester University Press. A case study allied to that of Hargreaves (1967).

Little, A. N. et al (1971) 'Do small classes help?' *New Society 18.*

Lunn, J. B. (1970) *Streaming in the Primary School*, National

Foundation for Educational Research. Not a sociological study.

Merton, R. K. (1957) *Social Theory and Social Structure,* Routledge & Kegan Paul.

Nash, R. (1973) *Classrooms Observed,* Routledge and Kegan Paul.

National Child Development Survey in Plowden Report (1967).

National Union of Teachers (1962) *The State of our Schools,* NUT.

Newson Report (1968) *See* Reports.

Nissel, M. ed. Social Trends, HMSO. An annual publication with many statistical examples of class chances.

Public Schools Commission (1968) *See* Reports.

Robbins Report (1963) *See* Reports.

Rosenthal, R. and *Jacobson, H.* (1968) *Pygmalion in the Classroom,* Holt. For critiques of this controversial study see R. Nash *Teacher Expectations and Pupil Learning,* Routledge & Kegan Paul, 1976, ch.3.

Sugarman, B. N. (1966) 'Social class and values . . ., *Sociological Review, 14.* See also his contribution to M. Craft, ed., *Family, Class and Education,* Longman, 1970.

Thomas, W. J. (1928) *The Child in America,* Knopf.

Vernon, P. E. ed., (1957) *Secondary Selection,* Methuen. A collection of papers.

Vernon, P. E. (1960) *Intelligence and Attainment Tests,* University of London Press. Chapter 2 presents the Hebb-Vernon model of intelligence.

Witkin, R. W. (1974) 'Social class influence on the . . . evaluation of school lessons' in S. J. Eggleston, ed., *Contemporary Research in the Sociology of Education,* Methuen.

Further reading

Cicourel A. V. and *Kitsuse, J. I.* (1963) *The Educational Decision Matters,* Bobbs-Merrill. An American study of school counsellors' part in social selection which unfortunately has no British equivalent.

Clark, B. R. (1961) 'The "cooling out" function in higher education', in Halsey, A. H., Floud, J. E. and Anderson C. A., eds, *Education, Economy and Society*, Free Press, 1961. A study of the way American junior college staff lower the ambitions of some students. There is no British equivalent.

Chapter 3 The family and education

Bernstein, Basil. For articles relating to Bernstein's work see:

Bernstein, B, and *Young, D. (1967) 'Social class differences in conceptions and uses of toys',* Sociology 1; reprinted in Bernstein, ed. *Class Codes and Control,* Routledge & Kegan Paul Vol. 2. 1972; *Jones, J.* and *Bernstein, B.* (1974) 'The preparation of the infant-school child', in W. Brandis and B. Bernstein, eds, *Selection and Control,* Routledge & Kegan Paul, Appendix;

(c) *Jones, J.* (1966) 'Social class and the under fives', *New Society, 221.*

Bernstein, B. and *Davies, B.* (1969) 'Some sociological comments' in, *Perspectives on Plowden,* ed. R.S. Peters Routledge & Kegan Paul, 1969.

Bronfenbrenner, U. (1958) 'Socialisation and social class through time and space', in *Reading in Social Psychology,* E.E. Maccoby *et al,* eds, Methuen. This charts some of the fashions in child rearing.

Craft, M.,ed. (1970) *Family, Class and Education,* Longman.

Crowther Report (1960) *see* Reports.

Douglas, J. W. B. (1964) *The Home and the School,* MacGibbon & Kee. Note chapters 5-8, 11 and 12.

Fletcher, R. (1966) *The Family and Marriage In Britain,* Penguin. Both this and Musgrove (1966) contain historical surveys of changes in the family.

Floud, J. E. (1954) 'The educational experience of the adult population of England and Wales', in D. V. Glass, ed. *Social Mobility*, Routledge & Kegan Paul.

Floud, J. E. (1961) 'Social class factors in educational achievement', in A. H. Halsey, ed. *Ability and Educational Opportunity*, OECD., 1961; reprinted in Craft, ed. (1970). Discusses the idea of the educogenic family.

Frazer, E. (1973) *The Home Environment and the School*, University of London Press. A Scottish study showing that children whose mothers went to work were not disadvantaged at schoolwork.

Goldthorpe, J. et al. (1967) 'The affluent worker and the thesis of embourgeoisement', *Sociology, 1.*

Jackson, B. and Marsden, D., (1962) *Education and the Working Class.*

Klein, J. (1965) *Samples from English Cultures*, Routledge & Kegan Paul. Especially vol. 2.

Musgrove, F. (1966) *The Family, Education and Society*, Routledge & Kegan Paul. This and Fletcher (1966) both contain historical surveys of changes in the family. Chapter 2, 'The good home' (reprinted in Craft, ed. 1970). This composite home is produced by the aggregation of some rather disparate studies.

Newson, J. and Newson, E. (1963) *Infant Care in an Urban Community*, Penguin, 1965.

Newson J. and Newson, (1968) *Four-Year-Olds in an Urban Community*, Penguin, 1970.

Newson, J. and Newson, E. (1976) *Seven-Year-Olds in the Home Environment*, Allen & Unwin.

Plowden Report (1967) *see* Reports. vol.2 includes Survey of parents of primary school children.

Swift, D. F. (1968) 'Social class and educational adaptation', in, H.J. Butcher, ed., *Educational Research in Britain*, University of London Press. A good review.

Toomey, D. (1970) 'Home centred working class parents', *Sociology, 3.*

Young, M. and McGeeney, P. (1968) *Learning Begins at Home*,

Education

Routledge & Kegan Paul. 1968 An experiment in home-school relations.

Young, M. and *Willmott, P.* (1960) *Family and Kinship in East London*, Routledge & Kegan Paul. Probably the best-known of British community studies.

Zweig, F. (1961) *The Worker in an Affluent Society*, Heinemann, 1961.

Further reading

Banks, O. and *Finlayson, D.* (1973) *Success and Failure in the Secondary School*, Methuen. Combined sociological and psychological research of boys in three schools. One interesting finding: successful boys in boys' schools tend not to be interested in girls.

Kahl, J. (1961) 'Common man boys', in A. H. Halsey *et al*, eds, *Education, Economy and Society*, Free Press, 1961. An American study. There may be British parallels to his 'get by' fathers of unambitious sons, and the 'get on' fathers of the ambitious.

Chapter 4 Language and education

Bernstein, Basil. Most of Bernstein's work on sociolinguistics is reported in:

Bernstein, B., ed. (1971–in progress) *Primary Socialization Language and Education*, Routledge & Kegan Paul, Ten volumes have been published so far, and a final concluding overview is promised. Most of the theoretical aspects are dealt with in:

Bernstein, B., ed. (1971, 1972, 1975) *Class Codes and Control*, 3 vols., Routledge & Kegan Paul.

Brandis, W. and *Henderson, D.* (1970) *Social Class, Language and Communication*, Routledge & Kegan Paul.

Cook-Gumperz, J. (1973) *A Study of Classs Differences in the Language of Maternal Control*, Routledge & Kegan Paul.

The last chapter is an extended critique of Bernstein's theoretical approach.

Robinson, W. P. and *Rackstraw, S.* (1972) *A Question of Answers*, Routledge and Kegan Paul.

Coulthard, M. (1969) 'A discussion of restricted and elaborated codes', *Educational Review*, 22.

Gahagan, D. M. and *Gahagan, G. A.* (1970) *Talk Reform*, Routledge & Kegan Paul.

Keddie, N.,ed. (1973) *Tinker, Tailor... the Myth of Cultural Deprivation*, Penguin.

Labov, W. (1972) 'The logic of non-standard English', in P. Gigloili, ed., *Language and Social Context*, Penguin, and in Keddie ed. *op cit.*

Lawton, D. (1968) *Social Class, Language and Education*, Routledge & Kegan Paul. Contains a resumé and critique of Bernstein's early work.

Lawton, D. (1970) 'Linguistic development and educability', in M. Craft, ed., *Family, Class and Education*, Longman. A useful review of Bernstein's work.

Rosen, H., (1972), *Language and Social Class*, Falling Wall Press. Rosen suggests Bernstein theories, implicitly if not explicitly, make working-class speech an inferior variety. More importantly, he points out that little evidence exists of language usage by men in their occupations: the nub of the social class.

Robinson, W. P., Language and Social Behaviour, Penguin, 1972. Chapters 8 and 9 are good resumés of Bernstein's work.

Trugill, P. (1974) *Sociolinguistics*, Penguin. A good introduction to social aspects of language.

Further reading

Cicourel, A.V. et al, (1974) *Language Use and School Performance*, Academic Press. These American studies follow an ethnomethodological approach which suggest that the social context of language is essential to its understanding. The general theory is given in A.V. Cicourel, *Cognitive Sociology*, Penguin, 1973.

Chapter 5 Schools as organisations

Ariès, P. (1973) *Centuries of Childhood*, Penguin. A social history.

Banks, O. (1955) *Parity and Prestige in English Secondary Education*, Routledge & Kegan Paul. Describes the processes of change at the turn of the century.

Bernstein, B. B., and *Davies, B.* (1969) 'Some sociological comments', in Peters R. S. ed. *Perspectives on Plowden*, Routledge & Kegan Paul. They refer to the 'horticultural model of the child'.

Chapman, J. (1971) 'School councils: in theory and practice', *Journal of Moral Education, 1.*

Coleman, J. S. (1961) *The Adolescent Society*, Free Press. For a critique see, M. Jahoda and N. Warren, 'The myths of youth', *Sociology of Education, 38,* 1965.

Dale, R. R. (1969) *Mixed or Single Sex Schools*, Routledge & Kegan Paul.

Easthope, G. (1975) *Community, Hierarchy and Open Education*, Routledge & Kegan Paul, ch. 6.

Eppel, E. M. and *Eppel, M.* (1966) *Adolescents and Morality*, Routledge & Kegan Paul.

Ford, J. (1970) *Social Class and the Comprehensive School*, Routledge & Kegan Paul.

Halsey, A. H. and *Gardner, L.* (1953) 'Selection for secondary education', *British Journal of Sociology 4.*

Hargreaves, D. H. (1967) *Social Relations in a Secondary School*, Routledge & Kegan Paul.

Hinings, C. R. et al (1967) 'An approach to the study of bureaucracy', *Sociology 1.* This and Pugh *et al* (1963) report aspects of a large-scale study of work organisation.

King, R.A. (1968) 'The headteacher and his authority', in, J. B.

Allen, ed. *Headship in the 1970s*, Blackwell.

King, R.A. (1969) *Values and Involvement in a Grammar School*, Routledge & Kegan Paul.

King, R.A. (1973) *School Organisation and Pupil Involvement*, Routledge & Kegan Paul. The only large-scale sociological study of British secondary schools. Pupil orientations are discussed in ch.3.

King, R.A. (1976) *School and College*, Routledge & Kegan Paul.

King, R. A. and Easthope, G. (1973) 'Social class and friendship choice in school', *Research in Education*, 9, Contains a resumé of the relevant research and original findings.

Lacey, C. (1970) *Hightown Grammar*, Manchester University Press.

Lunn, J. B. (1970) *Streaming in the Primary School*, National Foundation for Educational Research.

Mack, E. C. (1938) *Public Schools and British Opinion 1780–1860*, Methuen.

Murdock, G. and McCron, G. (1973) 'Scoobies, skins and contemporary pop', *New Society*, 23.

Murdock, G., and Phelps, G. (1972) 'Youth culture and the school revisited', *British Journal of Sociology*, 23.

Musgrove, F. (1964) *Youth and the Social Order*, Routledge & Kegan Paul.

Nash, R. (1973) *Classrooms Observed*, Routledge & Kegan Paul.

Opie, I. and Opie, P. (1961) *The Lore and Language of Children*, Oxford University Press. A fascinating collection by folklorists.

Plowden Report (1967) *see* Reports.

Pugh, D. S., *et al* (1963) 'A conceptual scheme for organisational analysis', *Administrative Science Quarterly*, 8.

Sugarman, B. N. (1967), 'Involvement in Youth Culture', *British Journal of Sociology*, 18

Veness, T. (1962) The School Leavers, Methuen.

Waller, W. (1932) *The Sociology of Teaching*, Wiley. This American classic has no British or modern counterpart.

Wilkinson, R. H. (1963) 'The gentleman ideal and the

maintenance of political elite', *Sociology of Education, 37.*

Wood, S. M. (1966) Uniform, its significance as a factor in role-relationships', *Sociological Review, 14.*

Further reading

Harré, R. (1975) 'The origins of social competance in a society', *Oxford Review of education, 1.* An exploration of the social world of children in school.

Hoyle, E. (1973) 'The study of schools as organisations', in H.J. Butcher and H.B. Port, eds. *Educational Research in Britain,* vol.3, University of London Press. A good review.

Warwick, D. (1974), Bureaucracy, Longman. Chapter 5 deals with education.

Chapter 6 Maintained Schools

Ashton, P. et al. (1975) *The Aims of Primary Education,* Macmillan.

Banks, O. (1955) *Parity and Prestige in Secondary Education,* Routledge & Kegan Paul.

Beloe Report (1960) *see* Reports.

Bennett, N. et al. (1976) *Teaching Styles and Pupil Progress,* Open Books. Especially ch.5.

Bernstein, B. B. (1975) 'Visible and invisible pedagogies' in, *Class Codes and Control,* vol.3, Routledge & Kegan Paul.

Blishen, E. (1969) *This Right Soft Lot,* Thames & Hudson.

Crowther Report (1960) *see* Reports.

Davis, R. (1967) *The Grammar School,* Penguin.

Department of Education and Science, Statistics of Education. The most important source of educational statistics.

Douglas, J. W. B. (1964) *The Home and the School,* MacGibbon and Kee.

Douglas, J. W. B., Ross, J. R. and *Simpson, H. R.* (1968) *All Our Future,* Davies.

Easthope, G. (1975) *Community, Hierarchy and Open Educa-*

tion, Routledge & Kegan Paul.

Floud, J. E. and *Halsey, A. H.* (1955) in Halsey, A. H., Floud, J. E., and Anderson, C. A. eds, *Education, Economy and Society,* Free Press.

Ford, J. (1970) *Social Class and the Comprehensive School,* Routledge & Kegan Paul.

Fry, J. D. (1974) 'O Level or CSE? The consequences of double entry', *Educational Research, 16.*

Holly, D. (1965) 'Profiting from a comprehensive school', *British Journal of Sociology, 16.*

Jackson, B. and *Marsden, D.* (1962) *Education and the Working Class,* Routledge & Kegan Paul.

King, R. A. (1969) *Values and Involvement in a Grammar School,* Routledge & Kegan Paul.

King, R. A. (1974) 'Short-course neighbourhood comprehensive schools', *Educational Review, 26.*

King, R. A. (1973) *School Organisation and Pupil Involvement,* Routledge & Kegan Paul.

King, R. A. (1976) *School and College,* Routledge & Kegan Paul.

King, R. A. All Things Bright and Beautiful?–Social Class and the Infant School, unpublished.

King, R. A. and *Easthope, G.* (1973) 'Social class and friendship choice in school', *Research in Education,4.*

Lacey, C. (1970) *Hightown Grammar,* Manchester University Press.

Lunn, J. B. (1970) *Streaming in the Primary School,* National Foundation for Educational Research.

Maclure, J. S. (1969) *Educational Documents 1816-1968,* Methuen. Contains extracts from the official reports referred to.

Marsden, D. (1969) 'Which comprehensive principle?' *Comprehensive Education, 13.*

Miller, T. W. (1958) *Values in the Comprehensive School,* Oliver & Boyd.

Monks, T. G. (1968) *Comprehensive Education in England and Wales,* National Foundation for Educational Research.

Education

Musgrove, F. and *Taylor, P. H.* (1969) *Society and the Teacher's Role*, Routledge & Kegan Paul.

Neave, G. (1975) *How They Fared*, Routledge & Kegan Paul.

Newson Report (1960) *see* Reports.

Plowden Report (1967) vol. 2: *see* Reports.

Pedley, R. (1970) *The Comprehensive School,* Penguin.

Robbins report (1963) *see* Reports; also Maclure (1969).

Ross, J. M. et al. (1972) *A Critical Appraisal of Comprehensive Education*, NFER.

Rubenstein, D. and *Simon, B.* (1969) *The Evolution of Comprehensive Education*, Routledge & Kegan Paul.

Sharp, R. and *Green, A.* (1975) *Education and Social Control*, Routledge & Kegan Paul.

Taylor, P. H. et al. (1974) *The English Sixth Form*, Routledge & Kegan Paul.

Taylor, W. (1963) *The Secondary Modern School*, Faber.

Turner, C. H. (1969) 'An organisational analysis of a secondary modern school', *Sociological Review*, 17.

Whitbread, N. (1972) *The Evolution of the Nursery – Infant School*, Routledge & Kegan Paul.

Further reading

Benn, C. and *Simon, B.* (1972) *Halfway There*, Penguin. A survey and review by two comprehensive school protagonists.

Monks, T. G. et al (1970) *Comprehensive Education in Action*, NFER. A collection of studies.

Welton, J. (1977) *Comprehensive Education and the Egalitarian Dream*, Pinter. A case study.

Chapter 7 Private Schools

Banks, O. (1955) *Parity and Prestige in English Secondary Education*, Routledge & Kegan Paul.

Goffman, E. (1969) Asylums, Penguin. See also his contribution

'The characteristics of total institutions', in E. Etzioni, ed., Holt, 1965. *Complex Organisations.*

Jackson, B. (1963) *Streaming: an education system in miniature*, Routledge & Kegan Paul.

Kalton, G. (1966) *The Public Schools: a factual survey*, Longman.

Lambert, R. et al (1975) *The Chance of a Lifetime?*, Weidenfeld and Nicolson. This is the major report of a large scale research project on all forms of boarding education. Chapter 12 gives an account of Lambert's experiments at Dartington School while its headmaster.

Mitchell, G. D. (1964) 'Education, ideology and social change in England', in G. K. Zollshan and W. Hirsch, eds. *Explorations in Social Change*, Routledge & Kegan Paul.

Public Schools Commission (1968, 1970) *see* Reports.

Simon, B. (1966) *Education and the Labour Movement*, vol. 2, Lawrence & Wishart. This is the source of the contemporary quotations.

Wakeford, J. (1969) *The Cloistered Elite*, Macmillan.

Weinberg, I. (1967) *The English Public Schools*, Atherton.

Wober, M. (1971) *English Girls' Boarding Schools*, Lane. Part of the Lambert research project (Lambert *et al*, 1975).

Further reading

Bishop, T.J.H. and *Wilkinson, R.* (1967) *Winchester and the Public School Elite*, Faber.

Lambert, R. et al (1969) *New Wine in Old Bottles?* Bell, A collection of studies including accounts of boys sponsored from maintained to public schools, with little satisfaction on their part.

Neill, A. S. (1962) *Summerhill*, Gollancz. The founder's account of a 'progressive' school.

Punch, M. (1974) 'The sociology of an anti-institution', *British Journal of Sociology*, 25. A study of Dartington School.

Wilkinson, R. (1964) *The Prefects* Oxford University Press. This compares public school education with that of the Chinese literatae studied by Weber.

Chapter 8 Further and higher education

Abbott, J. (1971) *Student Life in a Class Society*, Pergamon. Studies of the experience of university for students from different backgrounds.

Box, S. and *Ford, J.* (1967) 'Commitment to science: a solution to student marginality', *Sociology, 1.* A study of chemistry undergraduates.

Cotgrove, S. (1958) *Technical Education and Social Change*, Allen & Unwin.

Couper, M. E. (1965) 'Why some prefer CATS's', *New Society, 123.* The six Colleges of Advanced Technology become universities in the mid 1960s.

Halsey, A.H. and *Trow, M.* (1971) *The British Academics*, Faber. A large-scale study concentrating on university teachers.

Kelsall, R. K. et al (1970) *Six Years After*, Sheffield University.

Kelsall, R. K. et al. (1972) *Graduates: the sociology of an elite*, Methuen. Studies of the careers of a sample of university graduates.

King, R. A. (1976) *School and College: Studies of Post-Sixteen Education*, Routledge & Kegan Paul. Particularly chapters 7, 10 and 11.

Perkin, H. (1969) *Key Profession*, Routledge & Kegan Paul. A social history of the Association of University Teachers.

Robbins Report (1963) *see* Reports.

Shipman, M. (1967) 'Education and college culture', *British Journal of Sociology, 28.* A case study.

Taylor, W. (1969) *Society and the Education of Teachers*, Faber.

Tipton, B. F. A. (1973) *Conflict and Change in a Technical College*, Hutchinson. A case study.

Further reading

Butcher, H. J. and *Rudd, E., eds. (1971) Contemporary Problems in Higher Education*, McGraw-Hill. The contributions by E. Rudd and T. Burns deal with the student 'problems' of 1968.

Layard, R. et al. (1969) *The Impact of Robbins*, Penguin.

Chapter 9 Teachers and teaching

Allen, B. R.,ed. (1968) *Headship in the 1970s*, Blackwell.

Anderson, J. G. (1968) *Bureaucracy in Education*, Johns Hopkins Press.

Baron, G. and *Howell, D. A.* (1974) *The Government and Managment of Schools*, Athlone Press. A survey of governors and managers of maintained schools.

Bernbaum, G. (1974) 'Headmasters and schools', in J. Eggleston, ed. *Contemporary Research in the Sociology of Education* Methuen, 1974.

Bucher, R. and *Strauss, A. L.,* (1961) 'Professions in process', *American Journal of Sociology, 66.*

Burnham, P.S. (1968) 'The deputy head', Allen, ed.(1968). An empirical study.

Carter, M. P. (1966) *Into Work,* Penguin.

Channon, G. and *Delamont, S. eds.* (1975)*Frontiers of Classroom Research,* National Foundation for Educational Research. A number of methods and approaches are described by the contributors.

Coates, R. D. (1970) *Teachers' Union and Interest Group Politics,* Cambridge University Press.

Dale, R. R. (1966) 'Pupil-teacher relationship . . .', *British Journal of Education Psychology, 36.*

Delamont, S. (1976) 'Beyond Flanders' fields', in Stubbs and Delamont, eds.

Duggan, E. P. and *Stewart, W. A. C.,* (1970) *The Choice of Work Area of Teachers,* Sociological Review Monograph, *15*

Easthope, G. (1975) *Community, Hierarchy and Open education*, Routledge & Kegan Paul.

Etzioni, A. ed. (1964) *The Semi-Professionals and their Organisations*, Basic Books.

Grace, G. (1973) *Role Conflict and the Teacher*, Routledge & Kegan Paul. A selection appears in J. Eggleston, ed., *Contemporary Research in the Sociology of Education*, Methuen, 1974

Hargreaves, D. H. (1967) *Social relations in a Secondary School*, Routledge & Kegan Paul.

Hargreaves, D. H. (1972) 'Staffroom relationship', *New Society*, 492.

Hargreaves, D. H. et al. (1975) *Deviance in Classrooms*, Routledge & Kegan Paul. Deviance here refers to breaking teachers' rules.

Henry, J. (1966) *Culture Against Man*, Tavistock. Chapters 7 and 8.

Kalton, G. (1966) *The Public Schools: a factual survey*, Longman.

Keddie, N. (1971) 'Classroom knowledge', in M. F. D. Young, ed., *Knowledge and Control*, Macmillan.

Kelsall, R. K. et al. (1970) *Six Years After*, Sheffield University.

King, R. A. (1968) 'The headteacher and his authority', in Allen, ed. (1968).

King, R. A. (1969) *Values and Involvement in a Grammar School*, Routledge & Kegan Paul. Chapter 8.

King, R. A. (1973) *School Organisation and Pupil Involvement*, Routledge & Kegan Paul.

King, R. A. All Things Bright and Beautiful? Social Class and the infant school. (Unpublished).

McIntyre, D. et al. (1966) 'Social and educational variables . . .', *British Journal of Educational Psychology*, 34.

Manzer, R. A. (1970) *Teachers and Politics: the role of the NUT*, Manchester University Press. Conerns postwar activities.

Mays, J. B. et al. (1968) *School of Tomorrow*, Longman.

Musgrove, F. and *Taylor, P. H.* (1969) *Society and the teacher's Role*, Routledge & Kegan Paul.

Parry, N. and *Parry, J.* (1974) 'Teachers and professionalism; the failure of an occupational strategy', in M. Flude and J. Ahier,eds, *Educability, Schools and Ideology,* Croom Helm.

Perkin, H. (1967) *Key Profession,* Routledge & Kegan Paul.

Plowden Report (1967) *see* Reports. See the Survey of teachers in vol.2.

Robinson, P. E. D. (1974) 'An ethnography of classrooms', in Eggleston, (1974). See Grace (1973).

Simpson, R. L. and *Simpson, I. H.* (1964) 'Women and bureaucracy in the semi-professions', in Etzioni (1964).

Stubbs, M. and *Delamont, S., eds* (1976) *Explorations in Classroom Observation,* Wiley, 1976.

Tropp, A. (1957) *The School Teachers,* Heinemann. A social history of the NUT.

Waller, W. (1932) *The Sociology of Teaching,* Wiley.

Walker, R. and *Adelman, C.* (1976) 'Strawberries', in, Stubbs and Delamont, eds, (1976).

Weber, Max (1970) in P. Worsley,ed. *Modern Society,* Penguin.

Wilkinson, A. (1966) 'English in the training of teachers', *Universities Quarterly, 20.*

Further reading

King, E. W. (1973) 'The presentation of self in the classroom', *Educational Review,* 25. A speculative application of Goffman's dramaturgic sociology to primary school teachers.

Leggatt, T. (1970) 'Teaching as a profession', in J. A. Jackson, ed., *Professions and Professionalization,* Cambridge University Press.

Chapter 10 Trends and current problems.

Barnes, J. ed., (1975) *Educational Priority,* vol.3, HMSO.

Beetham, D. (1968) *Immigrant School Leavers and the Youth Employment Service in Birmingham,* Institute of Race Relations.

Education

Bernstein, B. (1970) 'Education cannot compensate for society', *New Society, 387.*

Bernstein, B. (1971) 'Open schools. Open society?', in B. R. Cosin *et al*, eds, *School and Society*, Routledge & Kegan Paul.

Bernstein, B. (1972) 'On the classification and framing of educational knowledge' in Bernstein, ed., Class Codes and Control, vol. 1, Routledge & Kegan Paul.

Bernstein, B. B. and *Davies, B.* (1969) 'Some sociological comments', in R. S. Peters, ed., *Perspectives in Plowden,* Routledge & Kegan Paul, 1969.

Brandis, W. and *Bernstein, B.* (1974) *Selection and Control,* Routledge & Kegan Paul.

Byrne, D. Williamson, W. and *Fletcher, B.* (1975) *The Poverty of Education*, Robertson.

Clark, B. R. (1962) *Educating the Expert Society*, Chandler.

Coard, B. (1971) *How the West Indian Child is Made Educationally Subnormal...*, New Beacon.

Coleman, J. S. (1966) *Equality of Educational Opportunity*, NCES Washington.

Crowther Report (1959) vol. 1: *see* Reports.

Durojaiye, S. M. (1971) 'Social context of immigrant pupils learning English', *Educational Research, 13.*

Gladwin, T. (1973) 'Culture and logical process', in Keddie, ed. (1973).

Grant, N. (1964) *Soviet education*, Penguin.

Halsey, A. H. (1974) Introduction to J.Payne, ed., *Educational Priority*, vol.2, HMSO.

Halsey, A. H. (1972-75) *Educational Priority*, HMSO, 5 vols.

Havighurst, R.J. (1961) 'Education and social mobility in four societies', in A.H. Halsey *et al*, eds, *Education, Economy and Society*, Free Press.

Jencks, C. et al, (1973) *Inequality*, Basic Books.

Keddie, N. (1973) Editor's Introduction to, *Tinker, Tailor. The Myth of Cultural Deprivation*, Penguin.

Kelsall, K. (1963) 'Getting on at the grammar', *Times Educational Supplement*, 15 March. Evidence of the closing of the class gap among early leavers.

King, R. A. (1971) 'Unequal access in education–sex and social class', *Social and Economic Administration, 5*; reprinted in R. Bell and K. Jones, *Education, Economy and Politics*, Parts 3 and 4, Open University, 1973.

King, R. A. (1974) 'Social class, educational attainment and provision', *Policy and Politics, 3.*

King, R. A. (1976) *School and College*, Routledge & Kegan Paul.

King, R. A. (1976) 'Bernstein's sociology of the school, some propositions tested', *British Journal of Sociology, 27.*

Little, A. N. and *Westergaard, J.* (1970) 'Educational opportunity and social selection in England and Wales', in M. Craft, ed., *Family, Class and Education*, Longman.

Midwinter, E. (1972) *Priority Education*, Penguin.

Plowden Report (1967) *see* Reports.

Stevenson, J. (1975) 'The nursery school language work', in Barnes, ed.(1975).

Tawney, R. H. (1952) *Equality*, Allen & Unwin.

Taylor, J. H. (1973) 'Newcastle upon Tyne. Asian pupils do better than whites', *British Journal of Sociology, 24.*

Thomas, W. I. (1928)*The Child in America*, Knopf.

Woodhead, M. (1976) *Intervening in Disadvantage,*, National Foundation for Educational Research.

Woods, J. (1975) 'The case study of a half-day language centre', in Barnes,ed.(1975).

Further reading

Bowker, G. (1968) *Education of Coloured Immigrants*, Longman.

Hargreaves, D. H. (1974) 'Deschoolers and new romantics', in M. Flude and J. Ahier, eds., *Education Schools and Ideology*, Croom Helm.

King, R. A. (1973) 'Education', in M. H. Cooper, ed. *Social Policy: A survey of recent developments*, Blackwell.

Rushton, J. and *Turner, J. D.* eds. (1975) *Education and Deprivation*, Manchester University Press.

Silver, H.ed., (1973) *Equal Opportunity in Education*, Methuen.

Index

Index